The Avenging All Blacks

Also available by J. B. G. Thomas

THE ROARING LIONS
THE MEN IN SCARLET
MEN, MATCHES AND MOMENTS
FIFTY TWO FAMOUS TRIES
SPRINGBOK INVASION

The Avenging All Blacks

The Story of the All Blacks' tour of the British Isles 1972-73

J. B. G. THOMAS

With a foreword by
CARWYN JAMES

PELHAM BOOKS

First published in Great Britain by
PELHAM BOOKS LTD
52 Bedford Square
London, W.C.1
1973

ISBN 0 7207 0678 5

Set and printed in Great Britain by
Tonbridge Printers Ltd, Peach Hall Works, Tonbridge, Kent
in Plantin ten on twelve point on paper supplied by
P. F. Bingham Ltd, and bound by James Burn
at Esher, Surrey

To John Dawes
and his Barbarians team
for the happiest moment
of the tour

Contents

PREFACE 11

FOREWORD BY CARWYN JAMES 13

1 The Judgement 17

2 The Men in Black 33

3 The Build-up 45

4 A Tough Start – Victory, Defeat and a Brawl 54

5 England and Ireland 70

6 Defeat and Precious Victory 86

7 Dial M for Murdoch 102

8 The Aftermath – and Murrayfield 109

9 Lost in the Fog 120

10 England, My England! 131

11 Return to Rodney Parade 138

12 Across the Sea to Ireland 146

13 The Lions Return 158

14 Finale in France 170

Appendix 1. Results and Details of Matches 179

Appendix 2. Appearances and Scorers 180

Illustrations

1 Smiles before the start of the tour *facing* 28

2 Michael Parkinson scores the first try of the tour 28

3 The victorious Llanelli team and reserves 29

4 One incident in the unpleasantness at Cardiff 29

5 Sid Going leads out the All Blacks against Ulster 44

6 John Burgess cheers on his team to victory 44

7 Grant Batty 45

8 Bryan Williams 45

9 Joe Karam about to score his hundredth point 45

10 The Tour Management 60

11 Glyn Turner dives over to score 60

12 Delme Thomas starts the movement that led to the disallowed Welsh try 61

13 Peter Whiting raises his arms in triumph 76

14 Referee Johnson disallows the 'try' by John Williams 76

15 Keith Murdoch 77

16 Sid Going draws in Doug Schick in the fog 77

17 An example of the difficult service received by Scottish scrum-half Ian MacCrae 108

18 Alex Wyllie storms his way through 108

19 England *v.* New Zealand at Twickenham 109

20 David Duckham out on his own 124

21 The 'wrestling match' in the game against Newport 124

22 Ian Kirkpatrick 125

23 Bob Burgess crosses the Neath/Aberavon line to score 125

24 The Irish XV that drew with the All Blacks 140

25 Fergus Slattery peels away 140

26 The All Blacks perform their Haka before the Barbarians' match 141

27 The Barbarian team that defeated the All Blacks 156

28 Slattery scores the Barbarians' second try 156

29 John Williams going flat out for the line 157

30 John Dawes being carried from the field in triumph 157

The author's thanks are due to the following whose copyright pictures are reproduced in this book: *Western Mail:* 2, 3, 10, 11, 12, 13, 14, 16, 21, 23, 26, 27, 28, 29, 80; *Thomson:* 1, 17, 18; *Central Press:* 4; *Mike Brett:* 6, 7, 8, 9, 15, 22; *Syndication International:* 19; *Sport & General:* 20; *Belfast Telegraph:* 24, 25; and also to all those other people whose help in obtaining pictures was so invaluable.

Preface

This was an unusual tour to cover, quite different from previous New Zealand tours. There were happy and sad moments and it was not quite like a Lions tour, especially that of 1971. Yet it was an important tour, all the more so because of the change in approach and attitudes of the New Zealanders.

The story of the tour occupied much travel, time and study, and for much of it I was handicapped by a broken arm, and so had to lean heavily on friends and members of my sports staff. All responded readily, especially colleague John Billot and secretary Jill Mathias.

When I could not get to certain matches, N.Z. pressman, Bob Howitt came to the rescue with shrewd, amusing but helpful comment. While the *Western Mail* photographers did a splendid job recording the highlights!

For the opportunity to cover the tour, my 18th major one, thanks are due to my Managing Director, my Editor and Thomson Newspapers, while the officials of the Rugby Unions and at the grounds where matches were played, as well as the liaison officers, were all most co-operative and helpful.

J. B. G. Thomas,

Cardiff 1973

Foreword

by Carwyn James

Hon. coach to the 1971 British Lions in New Zealand

I have always admired a nation like New Zealand who have worked out a pattern for themselves, a pattern which reflects national characteristics and national genius. I could never really understand, years ago, when people like R. H. Williams and Terry Davies returned from a tour 'down-under', and claimed that the national heroes in a country like New Zealand were the forwards. Every boy aspiring to fame wanted to be a Tiny White or a Whineray or a Meads. One now understands; it could not be otherwise.

The strength of New Zealand rugby is, and in fact always has been, in the power of its forwards, in the magnificent way they support and back one another up, the way they drive into the ruck and the next ruck, and in the contrived way they set up artificial platforms for delivery of the usable ball. The pattern is machine-like in its precision; it calls for dedication discipline; it is highly technical and teachable, and it is governed and controlled by the coaches who are very much in command of the game they know, and will not allow it to develop into an area which they do not comprehend or is not coachable.

Cut out the mistakes, we hear them say, get rid of the – pretty stuff, to hell with flair, with imagination, with genius, get on with your tackling, perfect the Garryowen, let's play our known game, the game which has brought us marvellous results and put us on the very top of World rugby and, or so it seems, don't let's enjoy it – too much. The approach, the rigid approach, suggests strength, but the pattern is so inhibiting that in the final analysis it is also the weakness of the game, and the weakness of the pattern.

It was in the Dragon Hotel, Swansea, that I first met the Seventh All Blacks, cheerful, smiling, obviously at peace with themselves and with the World. On the previous day, they had enjoyed their first taste of British rugby; they had found it wanting and they had hammered Western Counties by nearly 40 points, and, perhaps, even more important, their three-quarters had scored all their tries. A marvellous start to the tour, a great display by a team which has been billed by their own scribes as the 'worst ever to leave New Zealand', and in their first match they had already beaten one of the strongest sides in England.

While one felt happy for them (sadly I remembered Queensland only too well) one realised that perhaps it was not the best possible mental preparation for two hard games in Wales. The one at Stradey Park and the other at the Arms Park. Hard psychological blows were struck in these games and, for a long time, the All Blacks never really recovered their poise and it was only during the later stages of the tour, at Leicester and Neath in particular, did they again relax and play quality attacking rugby football. Hence, after their first week in Wales the withdrawal, the defensive mechanism, the reverting to type, their preoccupation with playing the known rigid stereotyped predictable game.

At best (and previous All Blacks sides displayed the qualities) it was fascinating, it was aggressive, coupled with skill and brilliance, and it was acceptable. Now, aggression with a minimum of the other virtues was not acceptable, and the Seventh All Blacks became involved in too many niggly incidents, not always their fault one admits, but their play, although often effective within limitations, was rarely brilliant and too often it was deadly dull. The pattern was simple, basic, inhibiting.

The greatest single influence on the tour was unquestionably Sid Going. He epitomises what is good and bad, what is strong and weak, for the New Zealand game. Time, and time again, Sid Going saved the tourists from defeat, he had the rare genius of suddenly being able to transform the whole game, he would turn defence into glorious attack, and he was always capable of switching on their powerful back row and getting the best out of his pack. It was always a sad occasion, for the New Zealand game, as for them, when Going had an off day, but even on his on days there were times when he was weak in the fundamental role of a scrum-half, that is, in his passing.

When he was concentrating on the running game and trying to breach the gain line near the set piece, never, during those moments, was anything further from his mind than the quality of his passing and often – as in the first half of the England match for instance – he threw out some dreadful passes. No wonder Burgess suffered, no wonder the threequarters became the forgotten men of the tour. Still, there were the days when Lin Colling played, a fine, fluent passer of the ball, and these were the days when we usually saw Robertson and Hurst and Sayers and Williams scoring tries and building up scores.

They are to be congratulated warmly on not losing an international match in the U.K. but the only game of the tour that will always be remembered in the hearts of people all round the World, will be the Baa-baas game, when the deficiences of the tour were exposed by a scratch side full of skilful players. In the end, skill matters more than power.

If the Seventh All Blacks were to re-start their tour, with the experience of the last three or four months behind them, they would surely develop into the most formidable unit.

I always felt that there was good potential in the party; one hopes for the future of New Zealand rugby, and for the future of the game, that this potential will be real, for the next season or two, and along different lines and culminating for a different pattern of play. The question facing New Zealand rugby thinkers now is this – can they afford to stick to their traditional pattern, play the Going type scrum-half and neglect the genius of generations of exciting players like Burgess, Robertson and Williams. I think not. New Zealand is rich in promising material and what is necessary now, I would have thought, is a man like Fred Allen, as a director of coaching, to rethink the pattern of the game in the two islands.

I would like to thank my good friend, J. B. G. Thomas, for asking me to write this foreword. I respect him as one of the foremost writers on the game, one of the most travelled rugby correspondents of all time, and one who has made the sporting pages of the *Western Mail* compulsive reading for so many of us. I got to know the travelling journalists well on the 1971 Lions tour; their contribution to the success of that tour was quite significant. And Bryn, in particular, a fellow Welshman, I would like to thank most sincerely for so much advice, help and guidance on that wonderful adventure.

1 *The Judgement*

The Seventh All Blacks will not be remembered in the same way as their predecessors, despite the controversy and criticism that surrounded their tour. They did not win the hearts of the followers of the game in the British Isles, or project the image of New Zealand at a time when it was most needed. They were over-introvert instead of extrovert, in a world of publicity and ballyhoo; they never seemed to bother about their public image, preferring to display a mild form of arrogance both on and off the field.

While this approach was not that of all the party, it was that of several members who mattered, and there developed a sort of 'love-hate' relationship with the crowds; often more hate than love! At times, the side was criticised more strongly and booed more loudly, than any previous touring team.

Somehow it lacked the social graces of the game and appeared to possess little idea of how to become popular and win friends. It appeared to arrive in this country with a 'chip' on its shoulder – one W.R.U. member called it a boulder, after trying to make conversation with a member of the team – but while one may argue that all this P.R. nonsense has nothing to do with the winning of matches on the field, it is quite important; more important than the players themselves realised.

Management plays an important part in the running of a tour and the image was created – one can only say from the outset – that Manager Ernie Todd and Bob Duff were too pleasant and too lenient with their side, and themselves courteous and retiring, in the sense that they did not project an image as did Smith and James in 1971.

Their final record in the British Isles of played 26, won 20, drawn two and lost four, with 521 points for and 227 against, is little inferior to that of the 1935–36 and 1953–54 sides, and they did not lose a test match against the four home countries, achieving three wins and a draw. Thus, in the words of Manager Todd, they achieved the objective he set before leaving New Zealand, 'We are out to win the four tests and, especially, to beat Wales!' They were the avenging All Blacks; a side determined to put right the defeats suffered at the hands and feet of the 1971 Lions. As most of those tourists were Welshmen, it was logical that they would make Wales the chief target. They did so and appeared not really to enjoy the tour until the Barbarians match, and then Ian Kirkpatrick did tell them in the dressing room after the game that it was time they drank to the health of John Dawes. Thus this fine Lions leader's remarkable image achieved in 1971 in New Zealand, still remained for what it was, a gentleman, sportsman, shrewd leader and good player.

Without wishing to appear too critical of the management, I do feel that Messrs Smith, James and Dawes would have succeeded in producing a better image for the Seventh All Blacks had they been in charge, and this has nothing to do with the relative playing strength of the sides they managed. The extra discipline, particularly where senior players were concerned, would have produced a better image. It is not easy to measure the loss of prestige suffered by N.Z. rugby in the British Isles through the 'acting up' and apparent arrogance of several players. What ever provocation they may claim, on and off the field – and certainly there was some, they should have disciplined themselves. Some of the players appeared rather 'big headed'; what they had got away with at home, they expected to do so on tour.

However much they may resent this criticism, let them first consider what the 1969–70 Springboks suffered in Britain and how well-behaved they were at all times. The All Blacks have no case for complaint at their treatment when one recalls the discipline and spirit of the Springboks, who were provoked everywhere they went, and were made to suffer night and day for the decisions of their government. Yet they behaved immaculately, on and off the field, and never put a foot wrong. How different from the All Blacks of 1972–73, and there are many in the British Isles who will never again give the same adulation to future All Black sides.

There has always been a close affinity between British and

New Zealand rugby, and especially so in Wales, even though the countries were great rivals. Outstanding names of past tours were household words. Gallacher, Wallace and Deans of 1905; Porter, Nicolls, Nepia, the Brownlies and Cooke of 1924; Manchester, Oliver, Caughey, Sadler, Mahoney and McLean of 1935; Saxton, Allen, Findlay and Scott of the Kiwis; Scott, Jarden, Davis, Stuart, Skinner and Tiny White of 1953; Meads, the Clarke brothers, Dick, Herewini, Briscoe, Nathan, Tremain and Whineray of 1963, and Meads, Lochore, Dick, MacRae, Gray, Nathan and Tremain of 1967. They were outstanding players, and even if Meads and company were rumbustious on the field, they showed a greater respect for their image off the field, than most of the players of 1972–73.

Perhaps, attitudes are changing in New Zealand, and the young men are not interested any longer in a love of the Mother Country. Perhaps the umbilical cord has been severed, never to be repaired again, and the tragic break has shown itself, first, in rugby football, in which the image of the country is projected more realistically than New Zealanders realise. It is a simple requirement... when guests in any country, be diplomatic towards its people and its customs, even though they may differ considerably from one's own.

How and why were the seeds of apparent discontent and misunderstanding sown? What brought about this dramatic change in attitude and relationships, that those who have been before on tour, must have appreciated were damaging, not only to rugby and future tours, but to New Zealand?

First, I feel the loss of successive tour series to the Springboks (away) and the Lions (at home), were almost a death blow to the pride and prestige of New Zealand rugby, and disturbed everyone within the country. Then, many senior players of experience retired and, suddenly, the selectors were left with a group of young players, many of them promising, plus a few hardened travellers, upon which to build their team for the British tour. In order to acclimatise the younger players, an internal tour was arranged for the All Blacks, something never done before but indicative of the intensity of the preparations.

On the internal tour, Jack Gleeson was manager and coach, and Bob Duff was a selector. Both wanted to go to Britain, naturally, and Duff won the place by a single vote. Gleeson was more of an extrovert and had won the press and the public over to his side. Duff was the experienced man, a former test captain and a disciple of the forward approach, while Gleeson believed in open, running rugby. New Zealand decided it would be forward rugby on tour.

When Todd and Duff were elected, they were both about to make their first visit to the British Isles, and of the players only Kirkpatrick as captain, Going as vice captain, Urlich and Williams had previously visited the British Isles to play rugby. Eight of the party had been to South Africa, on the 1970 tour, which proved such a disappointment, with wonderful provincial victories but defeat in the test series. On that team's return, great was the criticism of the manager and his assistant, but it was the beginning of an era in which the senior players on tour exerted too great an influence – and not always for the full benefit of the side.

One recalls that complete extrovert, Fred Allen, who had a superb side, and in this he was extremely fortunate because it contained brilliant and experienced players, in front and behind. He ruled them with a rod of iron, although willing to 'whoop it up' with them, and yet he was ready to defend them against criticism. He was lucky to have Charles Saxton as his manager in 1967 and even luckier not to have to face South Africa a second time in 1970, after suffering four test defeats as captain 1949, when the All Blacks team was split down the middle into two camps, and often played like it!

Following the retirement of Allen, Ivan Vodanovich took over the coaching and he was a man appointed by the Establishment, quite different from his extrovert predecessor. He seemed to obey the 'party line' and his success was meagre. This was as much due to the fading away of Allen's great team, as it was to Vodanovich's own limitations. The outstanding players were not replaced easily and Colin Meads, probably New Zealand's greatest forward, was expected to carry on for ever. A man of great determination and strength, he did more than anyone to try and repair the cracks in his country's fading power in the game. Having often criticised Meads for his excessive vigour, it would be churlish not to praise him for his magnificent service to his country on the rugby field AND his good behaviour off it. Indeed, the 1972–73 All Blacks needed a Meads, at the height of his power, for he had a rugby shrewdness and for a big man, a gentleness off the field that came with good breeding. One cannot recall Meads being a poor tourist off the field, in victory or defeat.

This was what the Seventh All Blacks lacked, as Going and Wyllie, two senior players and good footballers, did not seem able to supply the need and set a positive example which the younger members of the party could follow. Those with the party, and at home in New Zealand, may not agree with this assessment, but to my mind it sums up the situation even if one regrets saying it.

Every New Zealand player that ever played with Colin Meads, at home or abroad, looked up to him and respected him, since the 'Big Pinetree', though often a 'villain of the piece' on the field and a 'worrier and controller' of referees, as I have written before(!), had a magnetic influence upon young players, who followed him into battle as the children followed the Pied Piper. In 1971, at 35 years of age, he should not have been expected to play at top level, but he did; led his country, and got them to play good football in a happy series, and it was only a few stupid actions by some of his team, in NOT obeying some of his special orders, that caused incidents. He was immaculate in his approach and a modest captain, who conceded victory to Dawes without a grudge, and then as a sportsman retired from the scene of big rugby.

He could not have been expected to 'make' the 1972 side, despite a miraculous recovery from a motor accident, and with his passing from the field, there ended a long and notable era in New Zealand rugby history. Yet 1971 had to be avenged in 1972 and, following the successful and entertaining internal tour, the All Blacks crushed a poor Wallabies touring team in a three match test series by powerful forward play rather than back play. Nine man rugby proved so successful in terms of victory, with Bob Duff in command, that the pattern for the British tour was set.

Yet in this – and Barry John, who watched the third Wallabies test, pointed out that the All Blacks had no backs – who could really blame Duff for laying his tour plans upon the maxim of playing to his strength, at forward? It was in striking contrast to the approach of the 1971 Lions, but they had brilliant and experienced backs in Williams, Davies, Gibson, Dawes, Duckham, Bevan, John and Edwards, plus very able reserves. They had to build up their forward play to make full use of their backs, while Duff had to hope that his young backs would survive in 1972.

Thus one would admit that it was, basically, easier for James to create a flowing image than it was for Duff, and the New Zealander, quite rightly from his own point of view, played to his strength at forward, and especially through his big, mobile back row men in harness with Going, since all four took advantage of the continued British selection failure to realise that small back row forwards can no longer survive against bigger opponents. All four home countries were guilty of this and paid dearly for the error, no matter how good were the small men, since they could not be expected to dominate bigger opponents.

When asked what he had attempted most to achieve on tour, Duff commented, 'To put confidence into the players. It was a terribly young team when we set out. I styled my whole scheme of training and coaching to develop confidence, and even though I say it myself, I feel I succeeded.'

Yet I feel the whole tour was affected by the impact made upon the party by the defeat at Stradey Park in their second match, after a bright and breezy start at Gloucester against the Champion English county. Perhaps this first match, which promised to be hard one, proved too easy for the tourists. Their back row was able to dominate and there seemed every likelihood that they would do extremely well as a running side. Yet between the Saturday and the Tuesday, they felt the pressure of the build-up at Llanelli and they were bemused by the very special atmosphere; the tremendous partisanship of the crowd; the controlled vigour of the opposition, and the inspired coaching of Carwyn James.

There is no doubt that the rugby genius of Carwyn James produced a mental block in the All Blacks thinking and reaction for some time. In New Zealand they first respected him and then feared him, and he became a magician in the sense that Merlin was many years ago. They were never happy when he had anything to do with the opposition, and must count themselves fortunate that he did not have complete control of the Welsh XV and that John Dawes was not the captain.

The physical impact of Stradey Park was considerable and the All Blacks experienced a side taking the play to them and, immediately, the cry went up from the tourists and their camp followers that Llanelli were playing ten man rugby. Yet the mental impact was even greater, and the crowd's singing and the band's playing of 'Sospan Fach' and the famous rugby hymns appeared to them like a crusade. They did not like it, and although they had to admit that they were well beaten on the day and that Llanelli were the better side, they never recovered from the experience, and Carwyn James became a 'wicked magician' who weaved spells they could not break or even understand!

Then followed the 'disaster' at Cardiff where the tourists and the Club side engaged in 'feuding and fighting' throughout an afternoon that was a disgrace to the game. Cardiff read the 'riot act' to their players afterwards for they had not been instructed to play in the way they did but, obviously, their emotions boiled over. The All Blacks after Llanelli, decided they would not lose a successive match in Wales and were ready to 'retaliate'. No one can ever say who started it. No one should, but it was a physical clash of the worst order and there followed no really bad example again until the tragic exhibition of the All Blacks in the last 15 minutes of the Welsh test, when they seemed to opt out of the laws to stop the Welshmen taking the lead and winning the match.

This was their darkest moment of the tour and surely quite inexcusable. It revealed the basic attitude of the team as 'win at all costs'. Kirkpatrick was reported as saying, 'You never beat a Welsh team, you only score more points than them!' A dig at the Welsh no doubt, but on that day his side did NOT beat Wales, only scored more points. However, the impact of Llanelli and Cardiff brought forth perhaps the most naïve comment of the tour, made in *The Times* by Harold Power, which cloaked the identity of Terry McLean.

In *The Times* of November 24, he drew attention to the fact that British opposition to the All Blacks was being too well prepared and that it had 'become an even more serious business with the British than it was with the New Zealanders.' To this he added, 'Cynical New Zealanders cannot help laughing. Perhaps there ought to be some limit to enthusiasm; and a restraining factor ought to be an appreciation of the immutable fact that rugby after all is still a game – and amateur at that.'

After reading this, one better understood Terry McLean who, without realising it, had laid his finger on why the All Blacks did not really enjoy the tour. Firstly, they were surprised that the British, who generally offered a large number of easy matches to a touring team, should have 'grown up' in the game and prepared themselves as well as any New Zealand province, and secondly, they were trapped by their own approach.

Yet McLean had forgotten to mention in the article how New Zealand had 'crucified' Danie Craven's 1956 Springboks and how Waikato, who met them in the first match at Hamilton, had prepared for almost a year under the guidance of a brilliant coach in Dick Everest. I can recall McLean singing the praises of Everest on other occasions, but not in Britain in 1972!

If one compares Carwyn James and other coaches with Dick Everest, there can be no squeal from either side. New Zealand on this tour had more than a 'taste' of their own medicine and, quite frankly, there were some who did not enjoy it. One must be careful not to condemn those who adopt similar attitudes to oneself, as this can prove a dangerous practice. The Lions had to adopt N.Z. methods at the line-out in 1971 and go along with their referees, without complaint. It was a wise course of action and paid handsome dividends.

The selectivity of the N.Z. rugby memory was emphasised again by their press reaction to the Cardiff match; this even astounded me, a hardened critic of several tours. Young John Brooks, on tour for the first time, wrote a strange piece and highlighted the K.O. punch on Jeff Matheson by Cardiff forward, Ian Robinson. No one would suggest that it was a 'happy' gesture. Yet in 1969, Colin Meads took the law into his own hands, as did Robinson, and punched the jaw of Jeff Young, the Welsh hooker, because he had been pulling Ken Gray's jersey. Robinson says, and he is a truthful fellow, that he was being continually obstructed by Matheson at the line-out and other places.

The referee, Jake Young, was, in my opinion, far too lenient throughout the match as was Pat Murphy in 1969, but Young did not see Robinson's K.O. punch and one assumes that Murphy did not see the mighty swing of Meads. Two wrongs do not make a right, but the 'holier than thou' attitude, and the 'New Zealand are never wrong' belief, on the part of the New Zealand press, except for Bob Howitt, who wrote with amusing fairness in the *Western Mail*, was not on. I received weekly cuttings from New Zealand throughout the tour, and one can only assume that in many instances, the described happenings on the field were exaggerated.

One felt that the British press, for the most part, did lean over backwards not to be unkind to the tourists and suppressed much that was said and done. The Murdoch affair could not be kept quiet and once the news desks of the national papers got hold of the story, it spread like a prairie fire, as did the 'biting' story at Gisborne in 1966. When one suggests a press 'smear' campaign, one should have a good memory and think of past happenings. The Murdoch case was a sad one and perhaps he should not have been exposed to a tour in a highly sophisticated country by the national selectors who knew him well and it is they, indirectly, who were responsible for his tragic departure, as a Senior Sports Editor in Dunedin was quick to suggest.

Manager Todd did his best to plug the leaks in his ship, and even refused to give the whole story to his own pressmen. Murdoch was, I understand, 'ordered' home by the four home unions, and this was a wise decision, as the player must have experienced some difficulty in maintaining the requirements of the tour contract. When he left London he vanished into thin air, until at the end of the tour it was confirmed that he was in Australia. Until he returns to Dunedin and tells his side of the story, then only Manager Todd and the Chairman of the four home unions, John Tallent, can really give the 'whole' story which made the headlines in December 1972. It was 'big' news, if sad news, that Murdoch should become the first N.Z. player to be sent home.

One sensed that until this tragic happening there was a lack of discipline and humour in the side, for it had no smiling warmth, and there were frequent refusals to sign autographs for children, though one or two of the team, including Kirkpatrick, were notable exceptions. This did not endear the side to followers of the game. After the departure of Murdoch, the team eventually gathered itself together and behaved in a somewhat more friendly manner, but there were still some who would not communicate.

On any tour, there are occasional criticisms of referees, but in this side, Wyllie and Going complained far more than did the captain! They were real referee 'worriers', and Wyllie was told by Ernie Lewis at Redruth and Larry Lamb at Newport to stop talking or else . . . ! At the end of the Newport match Manager Todd, after hearing the complaints of certain players in his team and seeing that a hardened test player like Sid Going was nearly in tears after being penalised, let rip an outburst against Referee Lamb. This amused me as much as it did the referee, since the story of a New Zealand referee jumping in the air to award a dropped goal against Wales in 1969 was still fresh in my mind. At least one could see the amusing side of the picture.

Manager Todd's outburst brought forth a severe reprimand from John Reason of the *Daily Telegraph* who, through his match reports, did not appear to be charmed by the All Blacks at any time. He wrote, 'Mr. Todd should count his blessings. The All Blacks have won two internationals on this tour with the help of a generosity from referees which is never encountered by the Lions or the home countries when they go abroad.' Touché.

As a socialising team the Seventh All Blacks were poor, although some members of the party struggled hard and politely to make good the many deficiencies. I hope the younger players who did their stuff on tour will come again to the British Isles and, in different circumstances, really enjoy themselves among us. We are not as bad as the New Zealand press would have their country folk believe and the maxim of the 1971 Lions, who did 'what the Romans did', could have been adopted quite easily by the 1972 All Blacks, and it would have saved a great deal of heart-ache in New Zealand and the British Isles.

As the tour drew to its close, Manager Todd gave an interview in which he said his team had learned nothing from British rugby and this was followed by a forthright interview, in the *Western Mail*, with Ian Kirkpatrick in which he attacked the British Press and Welsh crowds. Before this Kirkpatrick and Going had given an interview to the '*New Zealand Herald*' alleging that British players were opting out of the laws and that Going was being wrongly penalised for not putting the ball straight into the set scrums. Kirkpatrick also suggested that Johnny Johnson, who refereed the Welsh test, was the best referee they had met on tour. I wonder why? The main criticisms of Kirkpatrick are interesting but more fierce than any ever made by any touring team captain about the British Press, as he did not spare them, even in the tone and quality of his language, but they were tough enough to accept it, and most of them refused to answer.

It is necessary to quote Kirkpatrick on this, although he may have changed his mind after reading what was written about his team after their approach at Neath and against the Barbarians: 'The Press coverage of the tour (and one assumes this includes the N.Z. representatives) has certainly annoyed the guys. It's been bad, it's been bloody false(?), it's been unfounded, it's been bloody untrue, and at times bloody disgraceful. The rugby reporters started putting the boot into us from Llanelli on. Whether it's because we have been winning the test matches, I don't know.'

These are hard words from a comparatively quiet player and person, normally most polite in approach and language. Vivian Jenkins had this comment to make upon the outburst in the *Sunday Times* ... 'Forgetting the adjectival monotony, perhaps the best thing to do in such circumstances is to raise an eyebrow, turn away and pretend one did not hear. The public no doubt will decide after what they have seen on TV. Rugby that produces this kind of reaction is perhaps better shelved for a decade or so.'

Wilfred Wooller, of the *Sunday Telegraph* had this to say, as a farewell comment, 'There is much to admire in New Zealand rugby but, at times, it has about as much humour as prime beef on the hoof. Sport without fun is like ham without eggs. Terribly boring if you have too much of it.'

David Frost in *The Guardian* wrote, 'The only yardstick by which followers in the British Isles can judge these All Blacks, is the play of previous visitors from New Zealand. Judged on that very high criterion, this on the whole has been a disappointing tour.'

John Reason, in the *Daily Telegraph*, finalised the tour as the ultimate in negatives and wrote, 'The tour which has just ended was a disappointment both from their point of view and the British. They did not play well, the British did not play well; they obviously did not enjoy themselves much, and the British did not much enjoy watching them.'

Reason continued, 'The 1972–73 All Blacks were not in the same class as their two previous touring teams, either in the forwards or the backs, but their forwards still had sufficient control of the ball from the line-out and the loose, to have played a much more ambitious game than they did.'

Harold Power (*alias* Terry McLean) in *The Times*, summarised as follows: 'The Seventh All Blacks may not be warmly remembered and because, being extremely young (average age 24½ years), they tended to react to criticism by withdrawing within themselves, they perhaps invited unkind words . . . In retrospect the British rugby may come to think a little more kindly about the team. To be coarse, the All Blacks did try to play their guts out. Not all touring teams have been so favoured.'

In contrast to these comments, Bob Howitt, one of the happiest of the whole party, had this to say after the Barbarians match, 'I didn't think it was possible for the 1971 Lions, coming together for a 'oncer' like this, to reproduce the dazzling rugby that made them such favourites in New Zealand. They not only did it . . . they did it better than ever. If the Lions can keep most of these marvellous players together, what a mighty tour they'll have in South Africa next year. That's a series I'd love to see!'

Howitt was generous in his praise of both sides, when deserved, throughout the tour and far less 'one-eyed' than some of his colleagues on both sides of the Press Box. He was quite prepared to say the All Blacks were in the wrong when it required saying, even when Going merited criticism.

In making a tactical appreciation of the All Blacks, one must first look to their forward strength which steadily improved as the tour progressed. Their scrummaging at the start was well below standard and their basic weakness at Llanelli, but when they adopted British methods of packing and binding, it improved.

They had trouble with their props and their feet placing, and the binding of their locks on the props but, once this was settled, they improved rapidly and developed a far better shove. Their line-out work improved and Peter Whiting at No. 5, grew in stature and won more possession, which was extremely valuable because the big forwards at the end of the line, especially Kirkpatrick, aided by Sutherland and Wyllie and the steadily improving young Stewart, generally had the better of their opponents.

Smiles before the start of the tour. Posing for photographs before a training session at Richmond two days after arrival in London

Michael Parkinson scores the first try of the tour, against Western Counties at Kingsholm, Gloucester

The victorious Llanelli team and reserves at Stradey Park. Back row (*left to right*): Selwyn Williams, P. Bennett, H. Peel (physiotherapist), T. David, A Crocker, D. Quinnell, Barry Llewelyn, Gareth Jenkins, R. Gravelle, Hefin Jenkins, R. Thomas, A. James, C. Charles, Bryan Llewelyn. Front Row: G. Ashby, Roger Davies, A. Hill, R. T. Bergiers, N. R. Gale, Delme Thomas (captain), Carwyn James (coach), John Williams, R. Hopkins, Meirion Davies

Just one incident in the unpleasantness at Cardiff: Cardiff's Keith James is on the ground while Williams, Sayers and Robertson 'discuss' the situation

Scown was given comparatively few chances but, as a loose forward, appeared better suited to British conditions, especially on the open side, and although New Zealand preferred fixed sides they did change their loose forward formation during matches. Wyllie was a much better scrummager than the heavier Sutherland, and when he was at Number eight, he worked hard, and was good at driving in the loose, scoring important tries against Scotland and Ireland.

The younger forwards made progress, for Graham Whiting and Kent Lambert were thrown in at the 'deep end' with the enforced absence of Murdoch and Matheson. Like McLauchlan and Lynch of the 1971 Lions, they came good, and should continue to serve their country well for many years. Macdonald proved his consistency as a lock and Andy Haden, a big fellow, made progress as a line-out jumper and learned to employ his weight and height in the loose, but Bevan Holmes had few opportunities with only nine appearances, as Wyllie and Sutherland were first choices for the No. 8 position. One assumes that in Graham Whiting, Lambert, Macdonald, Stewart and Scown, New Zealand has a good young nucleus for the future at forward. Again, all the forwards tackled and covered well in the loose and, as the tour went along, became more stable when they were 'turned' by opposing attackers, after revealing touches of panic in early matches. They covered their young backs exceedingly well.

Behind the scrum, Going was the boss. Of this there is no doubt and often, at half time, he would give the team talks. He preferred nine man rugby because he was expert at it and because, by international standards, he was an erratic passer of the ball. As a tactical kicker and runner from the scrum, line-out and ruck, he was expert while his covering and spoiling was first class. His close work with his back row forwards was frequently the most devastating attacking ploy of the team, but as for linking with his backs, he was rarely forthcoming.

He did not get the best out of Burgess, the leading mid-field attacker and preferred to have Ian Stevens at outside-half or first five eighth. This tended to stifle the young back division that had potential but was not encouraged. When Burgess and Colling were linked later in the tour, the side ran up big scores, as at Redruth, Leicester and Neath. When playing separately, one assumed they had been told to kick when in possession in their own half. As for Going's approach, effective as it was – except in the Barbarians match where he was spoiled and his passing was even more erratic – it was developed in the New Zealand era of nine and ten man rugby, and he was 'king' in his own province of North Auckland where he led his side astutely in this approach to a series of important Ranfurly Shield victories.

If New Zealand want to develop their back play then they must play a scrum-half other than Going, who will soon be 30 and possibly retiring from big rugby, or else stick to his 'narrow' approach and win matches with their forwards in the nine man style. One does not suggest that this is ineffective as the object is to win, but it is dull and unimaginative and I do feel, as do many others in New Zealand as well as Britain, that their young backs are deserving of greater consideration and involvement. One appreciates that nine man rugby, generally, forces the other side into errors, while 15 man rugby can produce more errors for one's own side!

At threequarter the All Blacks had two splendid wings in Bryan Williams and Grant Batty, but they received comparatively little encouragement and, had they been in a Lions side, would have got many more tries. Williams played 19 matches for seven tries and, as one of the world's outstanding wings, this was a poor return, and he spent too many afternoons shivering on the wing, defending and throwing the ball in. Batty scored 17 tries in the British Isles and was, for all his hasty temper, one of the discoveries of the tour and a most successful match winner.

The threequarters had to play second fiddle and this was made worse by the fact that Robertson suffered a long period of injury with a broken thumb and missed ten of the first 13 matches, but played in eight of the next 13. I liked this young man and believe he will become a strong attacker and help in a revival of back play when linked with Colling, Burgess and Hurst in midfield, and Williams and Batty on the wings. Unfortunately, the attacking full-back, Trevor Morris, never recovered from his injury in North America and the subsequent loss of form through a lack of match practice.

He was an attacking full-back as well as a place and drop kicker, and was badly missed because, although he was most adequately replaced at full-back and as a match-winning place kicker by Joe Karam, the other 'discovery' of the tour, the full-back position lacked the full attacking image in the modern idiom. Yet Karam won the Welsh test for the All Blacks, when another five minutes of the game would have seen the tourists overwhelmed. He deserves a big medal for his contribution to the tour and should play for his country for many, many years.

It is true that few British sides could play successful ten man rugby against the tourists but, occasionally, the tourists were beaten at their own game. The tourists believed it was their duty to win and not to please and, as one young player was reported as saying, 'We've not come on tour to win friends!' As a young side they did not possess the skill, ability or experience of their predecessors, yet they developed a determination and, in the Welsh match, this went far beyond the spirit of the game. They must have believed that it was worth it, even at the expense of damaging their image.

Ray Williams, the Welsh coach organiser, who is deeply interested in N.Z. rugby, commented that they achieved their goal but that there was more to rugby than merely winning. He confessed that he was sad because New Zealand played a very limited and unambitious type of football. I rather liked his comment . . . 'In New Zealand, victory is the name of the game, and the danger is that the pattern we have seen from the Seventh All Blacks will dominate rugby thinking there for the next five years. The way in which we win is equally important.'

The Barbarians match may have had an effect upon New Zealand thinking, but I doubt it, for it merely served to prove that the Lions, the best in the British Isles, were better in 1973 than the best of New Zealand. However, unless there are test matches in the British Isles, in future, between the Lions and the All Blacks, there remains the likelihood of the tourists avoiding defeat at the hands of the individual home countries. It is necessary for the Four Home Unions Tours Committee to amend this, and bring tours in Britain into line with those experienced by the Lions overseas. This is the most important lesson, administratively, to be learned from this tour since, tactically, there was little or nothing new in it. There is plenty of time to plan before the next visit of the All Blacks to the British Isles and the matter must receive immediate attention, for one cannot ignore the tremendous success and popularity and, indeed, high standard of play, produced by both sides in the Barbarians match.

Again, the quality of the Barbarians rugby would be adopted by a Lions side and, as it is so much more attractive and spell binding, particularly in its pace, power, elusiveness and accuracy in attack, it would succeed and ensure a continued hall mark of greatness for British rugby. It would help lift an overseas tour out of the doldrums in which this unfortunate Seventh All Blacks side frequently found itself. Again, it would prove an even greater financial success than was this one, and the point of money cannot be ignored.

So the All Blacks must come again. May they enjoy a happier tour, but they must play their part and 'give' more than did the Seventh All Blacks, for it is the people of the British Isles who made the tour possible. It is a game of the people, and their desires and views are always important.

We hope that the next visit will produce smiles and running rugby, and seek to emulate the 1935 All Blacks, Charles Saxton's Kiwis, and the 1971 Lions. The game has changed and will continue to change but its true spirit must not fade from the scene, or from the hearts and minds of rugby men, even at the expense of losing gracefully. This is a vital lesson of the tour which, at times, was not a credit to the game. However, the next visit of the British Lions to New Zealand in 1977 can help to put this right, especially if New Zealand, with its intense passions and seriousness for the game, survives the visit of the Springboks.

I hope that the young players in the Seventh All Blacks have not been 'scarred' too deeply by their experiences and will head a good and cheerful New Zealand team back to these shores for the Irish Centenary in 1974–75. If they smile off the field, and play running rugby on it, they will prove an outstanding success. It is up to them, for their hosts will make them most welcome!

2 *The Men in Black*

As the Seventh All Blacks were probably the most difficult of touring teams in the British Isles to get to know and understand – because of extremely poor PR work and a reticence about mixing with strangers – I hope I may be excused for not providing such a detailed analysis of each player, as in previous books. The British press do not live with touring teams, as do the New Zealand press on tour, and there is little 'haunting' and 'spying', or lurid stories told of their activities off-the-field.

What has been written and said about Keith Murdoch could certainly not have been suppressed, and thus the British press did not in anyway merit the unfortunate allegation by Manager Todd, that it was trying to 'smear' the All Blacks. I feel a large number of sincere, understanding British rugby writers resented this, and one could not blame them. Often they leaned over backwards not to upset the tourists and refused to investigate 'rumours' that could have led to other 'page one' stories.

One does not always agree with the technical opinions of one's colleagues, or they with mine, but I will not accept for one moment that any responsible rugby writer in this country went out of his way to condemn the Seventh All Blacks. They were criticised on results and approach; if several of the better-behaved and more pleasant members of the side suffered unfairly because of this, then it was unfortunate.

If I were asked why there was no love lost between the watching public, who make such tours possible, and the Seventh All Blacks, I would say it was because the latter had no humour in their play and at times lacked discipline. Maybe the two managers, who were extremely courteous to me and always ready to help, were too kind for the job. Most New Zealand sides need a whip-cracker!

Here are the Men in Black of 1972–73, and first the leader of the party:

ERNEST LAWRENCE TODD. Hon. Manager. Estate Agent. Aged 53 years.

Ernie Todd was a friendly fellow and I enjoyed talking to him. He should have gone to South Africa with the All Blacks in 1970 but had to wait his turn, as one can never be sure how the voting will go in the New Zealand Rugby Council, a powerful body. Yet his appointment was acclaimed as a good one, and he tried his best. I do not think he is as deserving of criticism for his failure to 'get tough' with his team, as are some of his senior players for not appearing as sporting and gentlemanly as himself.

A tour manager's job is a difficult one, and with a side younger than most in a highly sophisticated country, where values are changing all the time, and where the rugby approach was very different from that of 1967, no doubt Ernie Todd was surprised at what he saw and experienced. It may not have been what he expected!

Only on a few occasions did he burst into print and get the 'stick' – first for the 'smear' suggestion and then for the attack on Air Commodore Larry Lamb, the referee at Newport. He was wrongly quoted after the Barbarians match, for I spoke to him immediately afterwards, and he was delighted with the match and most complimentary towards the Barbarians, as well as praising his own players.

Although he served with the N.Z. Forces during the war; was an excellent back row forward who could have won a 'Fern' but for the war; an excellent N.Z. Council member and a good business man, Ernie Todd was not abrasive or a 'man of war'. He believed more in a policy of 'appeasement', and the fact that he was told to send Murdoch home hurt him deeply. Yet the incident called for strong measures, and my sympathy was much greater for Todd than it was for Murdoch. Todd had been let down and this is sad for a rugby team manager. It will be interesting to see how in time history will react to his leadership.

ROBERT HAMILTON DUFF (Canterbury). Assistant Manager and Coach. Accountant. Aged 47 years.

Many rugby officials told me after the tour that while Bob Duff was never rude, he was hard to communicate with, and although I did not find this to be true, he is a quiet man. He has been a fine player, an effective coach and a sound official during his long career in the game.

He was a big lock forward, a bigger man in his playing days than during the tour, and for twelve years served Canterbury well – and that province has produced some good forwards. He was an All Black from 1951 to 1956 and led the All Blacks in two memorable tests in the fierce series of 1956 against the Springboks.

Yet like Ernie Todd, he was not an extrovert in the Fred Allen manner, and never a 'man of war' – at least I never found him so. The players appeared to like him even if, occasionally, a senior player argued with him. He got on with the job and withstood criticism, from outside and inside his party, of his coaching and training methods.

Some suggested he was 'old fashioned' but he had, in the main, a young side and he decided, long before the first match, that he would play to its strengths: at forward and Sid Going. He was observant, and wise enough to adopt ideas in British forward play, especially scrummaging, to improve that of his own side.

He did not criticise opponents or overpraise his own side. He got on with his job quietly and, if deeply disturbed by the defeat at Llanelli, soon recovered. I can only say that I enjoyed chatting to him about rugby and New Zealand, and appreciated his friendship and courtesy. Maybe the team needed an 'extrovert' to coach them, but he could not have worked harder or been more devoted than Bob Duff.

IAN ANDREW KIRKPATRICK (Poverty Bay). Captain. Flanker. Aged 25. 6 ft. 2 in. 16 st. 2 lb. Farmer.

An outstanding flank forward and a courteous tourist, but appeared to be too gentlemanly a personality to keep some senior players in check. He believed in playing a straightforward game and never was guilty of any misdemeanours on or off the field. Made 20 appearances out of 26 in Britain which was one more than John Dawes in N.Z. in 1971. Enjoyed pointed out opposing errors to referees and should have encouraged the side to run more, as he did himself in close unison with Going and the back row. Had Wyllie as a rival for the captaincy before the tour started, and the N.Z. press maintained that Wyllie was the 'field captain'. Kirkpatrick has appeared in 23 tests and will make many more as he has years left in game, while consistency of form is his hallmark. He said many harsh things about the Welsh and British in a special *Western Mail* interview before he left for France, but would still be welcomed back to the British Isles as he is a genuine prototype New Zealander of the future.

TREVOR JAMES MORRIS (Nelson Bays), full-back. Aged 30. 5 ft. 10½ in. 12 st. 7 lb. School teacher.

Unluckiest player on the tour as he had only eight matches although he set off from N.Z. as first choice full-back and place kicker. Suffered a leg injury in North America before reaching Britain and missed the first seven matches. After that his form was erratic but some days he showed what a fine player he was. Obviously, his injury and loss of form was a big blow to the tourists. Excellent sportsman and most likeable of tourists who could have been outstanding but fortunately Karam made good in his absence.

JOSEPH FRANCIS KARAM (Wellington), full-back. Aged 20. 5 ft. 8 in. 12 st. 8 lb. Salesman.

Played on wing for Manawatu against Lions in 1971 and then moved to Wellington for 1972. Was THE discovery of tour when he took over important job from injured Trevor Morris at start and showed remarkable consistency. Excellent place kicker, his five penalties beat Wales, and also a sound line kicker although not too venturesome in attack, in accordance with side's tactical policy. In 17 matches, including all tests and Barbarians match, Karam scored 125 points and won several of the matches. Sound in defence he was an extremely popular tourist.

GRANT BERNARD BATTY (Wellington), wing. Aged 20. 5 ft. 5½ in. 11 st. Clerk.

The ball-of-fire man and, next to Going, the man the crowds loved to boo! Had plenty of ability and pace but his fiery temper often got him into trouble, and he especially hated being tackled. He was top try scorer in the British Isles, making

11 of his 18 appearances on the left-wing. Was a fierce competitor and a remarkable tackler for his size but was far from being the most popular tourist, when he could have been the most popular of all. Will be first choice on the wing for N.Z. for many years.

DUNCAN ALISTER HALES (Canterbury), wing. Aged 24. 5 ft. 10 in. 13 st. Student.

A most useful player at centre or wing who made 15 appearances, including the vital test against Wales when Robertson was injured. Attracted attention during 1972 internal tour and worked hard for his five tries. Well built and resourceful, he was a first class defender and runner in.

GEORGE RUPUHA SKUDDER (Waikato), wing. Aged 24. 5 ft. 10½ in. 12 st. 13 lb. School teacher.

Did not have a happy tour because of persistent hamstring injury. Missed first five matches but trained under orders when he should have been rested, and played in several hard matches when back play was not the order of the day. Scored three tries in ten matches but was never in the class of Williams and Batty, although an extremely quiet and courteous tourist.

BRYAN GEORGE WILLIAMS (Auckland), wing. Aged 21. 5 ft. 10½ in. 13 st. 5 lb. Law student.

Before start of 1971 Lions tour was regarded as one of great N.Z. wings following successful trip of S.A. in previous year. Did not shine against Lions owing to injuries but did better in 1972 and was regarded as No. 1 wing. Played mostly on the right, but should have been on left where side step would have been more effective. Was strong, and showed in Barbarians match how much better he would have been in a running side. Was also excellent place kicker. In 19 matches he scored seven tries but would have gathered double that number outside the 1971 Lions midfield players.

IAN ARCHIBALD HURST (Canterbury), centre. Aged 21. 5 ft. 11 in. 13 st. Farm management student.

Another surprise selection for the tour and appeared in only four of the first 15 matches but then in eight of last 11 as he showed good form, especially as midfield partner to Robertson and Burgess, completing what was the best attacking triangle in the side. Won first cap against Ireland and should win many more to help N.Z. recapture its real back play and effectiveness in midfield, despite coming from province famous for hard forwards.

BRUCE JOHN ROBERTSON (Counties), centre. Aged 20. 6 ft. 1 in. 13 st. 3 lb. Student teacher.

Could have been the outstanding back of the tour but for injuries and the side's approach. He will become one of N.Z.'s leading midfield players in the years ahead. Broke thumb in Cardiff match, then suffered succession of hamstring injuries and did well to make 11 appearances out of a possible 16, as he was unfit for ten matches after the Cardiff game. Has natural ability and when experienced will make fuller use of his turn of speed, good hands and eye for an opening. Was excellent tourist and made friends easily. Appeared against Scotland, England, Ireland and Barbarians.

ROSS MICHAEL PARKINSON (Poverty Bay), second five-eighth. Aged 23. 6ft. 12 st. 7 lb. Freezing worker.

Made 11 appearances at second five eighth and was in the first three tests against Wales, Scotland and England before being replaced by Hurst, in attempt to improve side's attacking strength. Hard player and fine defender but suffered from the side's approach. Will benefit when N.Z. really run the ball as they did on rare occasions, notably at Gloucester, Leicester and Neath.

MARK SAYERS (Wellington), second five-eighth. Aged 24. 6 ft. 12 st. 7 lb. School teacher.

Made 13 appearances, generally at second five-eighth (inside centre), and was useful performer having had good season with province. He impressed occasionally with outside break but like all midfield players in party suffered from nine man rugby. Manager Todd said British sides would not let his midfield players run, but Going's tactics rarely allowed them to do so, and young players like Sayers suffered.

ROBERT EDWARD BURGESS (Manawatu), first five-eighth. Aged 23. 5 ft. 9 in. 11 st. 2 lb. Student.

An outstanding player in 1971 test series against Lions and his long hair was no guide to his fine ability as an attacking player. An excellent tourist, intelligent and thoughtful off the field with all the courtesies. Lost form in a side that was without flair, but returned later to regain test place. Appeared against Wales and Ireland as well as Barbarians, and dealt most ably with Going's erratic service. Made 16 appearances and in these were the four defeats of the side but had the team employed his approach throughout, it would have been more popular.

IAN NEAL STEVENS (Wellington), first five-eighth. Aged 24. 5 ft. 9 in. 12 st. 3 lb. Clerk.

One of the surprise selections for the tour, as he was a scrum-half until the 1972 season in New Zealand. Was better able to play second fiddle to Going than the more creative Burgess, and was given Scottish and England tests before Burgess returned to favour. Useful footballer but not really test standard at outside-half, although he did not let the side down in their chosen approach.

GEORGE LINDSAY COLLING (Otago), scrum-half. Aged 25. 5 ft. 9 in. 11 st. Company representative.

Was an outstanding scrum-half for province against Lions and worthy choice for tour. Colling was a long spin-passer of the ball but not ideally suited to nine man rugby. When partnered with Burgess later in the tour, the side was always more attractive. An excellent tourist and likeable player who deserves full test cap. Replaced injured Going during second half of Barbarians match, and made 16 appearances during tour.

SIDNEY MILTON GOING (North Auckland), scrum-half. Aged 27. 5 ft. 6¾ in. 12 st. 5 lb. Farmer.

The shrewdest rugby player in the side but not, by many a mile, the most popular member of the party, on or off the field. Vastly experienced, strong, clever, shrewd and expert at nine man rugby and linking with back row. Not a good passer of the ball, he was surprised when British referees eventually took a dislike to his method of scrum put-in. Beautiful tactical kicker and spoiler; strong on individual burst, but met

'Waterloo' against Gareth Edwards when not one hundred per cent fit, and should have withdrawn against Barbarians. One felt he could have done so much more for side in P.R. work, with his considerable touring experience, but he remained uncommunicative when both tour and Kirkpatrick needed help. Made 16 appearances and led side on few occasions.

BEVAN HOLMES (North Auckland), No. 8. Aged 26. 6ft. 2 in. 15 st. School teacher.

Never really had the chance to establish himself with only nine appearances, and in face of the challenge of Sutherland and Wyllie. Useful player but we never really saw best of him, as when playing for North Auckland. Toured S.A. in 1970. but never awarded full test place, although still young enough to get a cap when Sutherland and Wyllie retire.

ALAN RICHARD SUTHERLAND (Marlborough), No. 8. Aged 28. 6 ft. 3 in. 17 st. Company representative.

Clever back row forward, particularly in defence, but not as good a scrummager as Grizz Wyllie. Was injured after first test against Lions in 1971 but was a strong player on this tour, although one felt he faded a little towards the end through illness and injury. Heavy for loose forward but extremely good at line-out. Made 14 appearances, and all but two were at No. 8.

ALISTAIR IAN SCOWN (Taranaki), flanker. Aged 23. 6 ft. 1½ in. 15 st. Farmer.

Made reputation in 1972 as flanker after early period on the wing. Played against Lions for province in 1971 and then against Australians in tests of the following year. Made 11 tour appearances but found difficulty in adjusting, at first, on the field, although a quiet, pleasant tourist. Got a test against Scotland when Sutherland fell out, and again in the Barbarians match. Young enough to win many more test caps.

KENNETH WILLIAM STEWART (Southland), flanker. Aged 19. 6 ft. 1½ in. 14 st. Farmer.

Was spotted at Invercargill, while still at school, in 1971, playing for his province against the Lions. Ear-marked for the big time, he was chosen for the tour at age of 19 and celebrated his 20th birthday in Britain. Good player with a promising future, he survived and learned much with the big men during his 10 appearances.

ALEXANDER JOHN WYLLIE (Canterbury), flanker. Aged 27. 6 ft. 1 in. 16 st. Farmer.

Was considered the 'wild man' of 1971 Lions tour but did notable job as leader of Canterbury in 1972 and was runner up for captaincy of Seventh All Blacks. Outspoken, on and off field, and chief referee 'worrier', he exerted tremendous influence on the tour, especially on the tactical approach and was christened the 'field captain' by the N.Z. press. Excellent forward at No. 8 or on flank, but lacked humour in his play.

IAN MATHESON ELIASON (Taranaki), lock. Aged 26. 6 ft. 2 in. 16 st. Farmer.

Made only four appearances in first 15 matches and was long time adjusting to British approach, especially at line-out. Then he improved and played in five of the last 11 games, but, obviously, as fourth lock he had fewer chances bearing in mind team's need to play Whiting and Macdonald together in ten matches. Played on internal tour in 1972 and works hard for his province where forward play is generally vigorous.

ANDREW MAXWELL HADEN (Auckland), lock. Aged 22. 6 ft. 6½ in. 17 st. 7 lb. University student.

The biggest man in the side, being a little heavier than Auckland colleague Peter Whiting. Was raw at first and surprised by all that happened at Llanelli, but developed to make 13 appearances. He learned to use his physical skills for the full benefit of winning possession. Could become a powerful forward, and a big one, to form future hard core of N.Z. test pack.

HAMISH HUGH MACDONALD (Canterbury), lock. Aged 24. 6 ft. 3 in. 15 st. Farmer.

One of the successes of the tour, on and off the field, as a quiet, hard-working player and polite tourist. He and Peter Whiting were test locks – and effective ones. Made 14 appearances, three less than Whiting, but was splendid lock forward, good at line-out and rucks. Should hold test place for several years to come with his modest consistency.

PETER JOHN WHITING (Auckland), lock. Aged 26. 6 ft. 6½ in. 16 st. 11 lb. School teacher.

Was raw and rough when he first appeared in the 1971 test series against Lions but had done well for Auckland. Tangled with Gordon Brown in the last test of 1971 and was not popular then, but showed more restraint on this tour, although working hard at line-out and rucks. Expert at playing up to referees at line-out and shared in 'Cornish wrestling match' with Lyn Jones at Newport. Was hard core of side but not yet in Meads class for quality.

KENT KING LAMBERT (Manawatu), prop. Aged 20. 5 ft. 11½ in. 16 st. Student.

Was a beginner in real art of propping at start of tour as one would not expect a 20 year old to be a 'master'. However, force of circumstances required him to concentrate and the injury to Matheson in Scotland gave him his big chance. He took it well to survive against McLauchlan and Carmichael. In the end he played 13 matches in British Isles with three tests and the Barbarians match. Another player who should serve N.Z. well for many years.

JEFFREY DAVID MATHESON (Otago), prop. Aged 24. 5 ft. 11½ in. 15 st. 9 lb. Farmer.

Injured in ninth appearance of tour, when early in Scottish match he sprung his ribs, and was forced to drop out of side and recover in London before returning home with a painful injury. He was a first-class prop – another from Otago – and pleasant tourist but got 'felled' in Cardiff match with upper-cut from Robinson, after continuous and annoying obstruction on that player – the treatment N.Z. players apparently respect!

GRAHAM JOHN WHITING (King Country), prop. Aged 23. 6 ft. 3½ in. 17 st. 7 lb. Insurance agent.

Played against Wallabies in 1972 after proving himself on internal N.Z. tour. Did not excel at first in Britain, but when Murdoch disappeared, he took the added responsibility seriously and developed into a first class prop, holding his own, in partnership with Lambert, against the Scottish test pair, and in the Barbarian's match. Vigorous, good on peel-off and ready to retaliate! Should serve N.Z. well for several years.

RANGITANE WILL NORTON (Canterbury), hooker. Aged 29. 6 ft. 13 st. 4 lb. Bank officer.

Played so hard and well against Lions in 1971 for Maoris and Canterbury that he won test place ahead of Urlich. Quick striker and vigorous forward, especially good at marking scrum halves from line-out, where he breaks quickly from front end. Was first test choice on tour, playing in all four internationals, and making 12 appearances, several of which were with pain killing injection for achilles tendon trouble.

RONALD ANTHONY URLICH (Auckland), hooker. Aged 28. 6 ft. 14 st. Draughtsman.

Came as second choice to Tane Norton who replaced him for Lions tour in 1971. Toured S.A. in 1970 and in R.F.U. Centenary Celebrations. Good, strong, lively player who made 14 appearances to 12 by Norton in British Isles, and got plum match against Barbarians in which he lost only one tight head and enjoyed lose play. Has been outstanding in successful Auckland side.

LINDSAY CLARK (Otago), prop. Aged 30. 6 ft. 15 st. Company representative.

This sound, hard-working, likeable prop, had the unenviable task of flying over as replacement for the unfortunate Murdoch, but did as good a job, on and off the field, as the 'missing one'. He made five appearances in British Isles but was injured towards end of tour. Clark came from Otago, where good fast forwards are produced, and did not let the province down, although he never dreamed he would 'make it'!

ALISTAIR 'SANDY' McNICOL (Wanganui), prop. Aged 27. 6 ft. 2 in. 16 st. 12 lb.

Came as replacement for injured Jeff Matheson and played in three matches in British Isles at Newport, Cork and Neath, and thus had good taste of earthy British approach, but answered requirements with sound displays as befitting experienced campaigner from Wanganui.

KEITH MURDOCH (Otago), prop. Aged 27 6 ft. 17 st. 4 lb. Farmer.

Did not appear against British Lions in 1971 although regarded then as toughest forward in New Zealand, following S.A. tour in 1970 and exploits with Otago. Chosen for province and three tests against Lions but never appeared. Said to be the key figure 'psychologically' in Seventh All Blacks front row and was ball of fire, on and off field, until the Welsh match, in which he scored N.Z. try, but was then sent home for misbehaviour in team's hotel. 'An uncompromising character', was the official description of him but on leaving London after Welsh match he was not seen again and is now known as the *Marie Celeste* of rugby football!

In addition, the party included five press members, four of whom were here with full tour for the first time, two cameramen, and one N.Z.B.C. commentator. A baggage master and hon. secretary travelled with the team, and were provided by the four home unions, while each home union provided a liaison officer. The party travelled by 'plane, train and coach, stayed at the best hotels, and were provided with the opportunity of studying the British Isles and its people. Only they can say whether they enjoyed it, but I have my doubts, although nine of the side returned to play in the Scottish Centenary matches in March and April.

Many of them may come again. I hope so and, perhaps, next time, they will enjoy themselves more, both on and off the field. All overseas rugby tours are what the members of the visiting party make them. There can be no other way!

Sid Going leads out the All Blacks against Ulster at Ravenhill, Belfast, under the watchful eyes of the security forces

The North West Counties coach, John Burgess, cheers on his team to their historic victory over the All Blacks

The wings who thrilled British crowds with some marvellous running whenever they were given the chance: Grant Batty (*left*) and Bryan Williams. One of the tour's great successes: Joe Karam (*below*) about to score his hundredth point, against Midlands Counties East

3 *The Build-up*

The Kiwi challenge of 1972–73 was launched the moment the victorious British Lions roared into the sky at Auckland Airport late on Sunday night, August 15, 1971. As the New Zealand officials waved goodbye and drove back to their homes and hotels in the city, they said to themselves: 'Now we must prepare for 1972–73 and victory in the British Isles!' The Lions' success had disturbed the whole of New Zealand and the second successive defeat in a test series was too much for a proud, independent, sports-loving people for whom rugby football is a way of life.

The Lions became the first touring team to win a full test series in New Zealand since 1937 and the first British side to prove itself successful in the two Islands. The tour proved two things that were to be discussed right up to the arrival of the 1972 All Blacks. First, the fact that New Zealand rugby was no longer invincible at home and had stood still, content in its own methods. Secondly, the tour revealed that British Rugby had improved beyond measure, and had moved ahead of new Zealand rugby, tactically, and in application of modern ideas, especially coaching and squad training.

It was the British ideas and the superb team work, in defence and attack, that revealed New Zealand rugby as stereotyped and inflexible; content with creating situations to win the ball but rarely being able to make full use of it when it was obtained. The British had taught themselves to scrummage correctly and to combat the All Blacks at the line-out; to get to the rucks and fight for the ball, to move it quickly to the wings and to counter attack, especially from full-back. They also possessed magnificently accurate and consistent place kickers. In addition, they had an outstanding captain, coach and match winner, plus an unshakeable team spirit and they deserved to succeed. All four countries were faithfully united and the Lions were a team.

The critics hit New Zealand rugby hard and no writer spared the N.Z.R.U., with its old fashioned ideas and its refusal to change its approach to the game. There was call for change and later the N.Z.R.U. were to write to the Welsh Rugby Union, seeking details of that Union's successful coaching system. What had really happened was that New Zealand had become reactionary as a result of continued success. The Fred Allen era was over, and the success of the power pack with its continuous supply of the ball, plus four orthodox back movements and accurate goal kicking, could not continue unchallenged.

In New Zealand, it had seemed a foregone conclusion that each home test series would be won but the decisive two match series against Wales was the last great moment of triumph for the N.Z. approach. The Welsh returned home, bitter in defeat and determined to avenge it, while New Zealand set off for South Africa in 1970, to experience their own moment of truth. Their approach was mastered as the Springboks overcame them in a hard fought test series.

Amazingly successful in the provincial matches, while running up large scores, the All Blacks became extremely confident, too confident, and the Springboks, matching them in the tight-loose play and set pieces, were able to destroy them in mid-field. Their persistent and predictable attempts to set up second phase play were contained easily by powerful tackling and intensive back-row play. It was often hard and rugged, with outbursts of rough play, but the All Blacks' methods were no longer successful.

Yet again, the All Blacks had failed in their ambition to win a series in South Africa, and 1928, 1949, 1960 and 1970 had seen them held (2–2), (4–0), (2–1) and (2–1). The burning ambition to win in South Africa, as the Springboks had won in New Zealand in 1937, is still unfulfilled. This defeat abroad was hard enough to take but worse was to follow in 1971, at home, and the success of the Lions launched a revolution.

New Zealand critics and members of the public and, indeed, representatives within the corridors of rugby power, were seeking 'heads' after the Lions returned home. Ivan Vodanovich, a pleasant and amiable fellow, intensely devoted to his job, fell out of favour and he could have stepped down, such was the opposition against him, not as a person but for his failure as a coach. One has to live in New Zealand through a tour to realise the burden carried by a coach – if he is successful, he is 'king', but failure is not tolerated.

That was why Fred Allen was clever in retiring when he did from this onerous post, for had he gone to South Africa in 1970 as assistant manager and coach, he may well have lost his popularity, as he had when captain of the 1949 All Blacks in South Africa. He said of that ill-fated 1949 tour, 'They had the gallows up for me when the ship reached Wellington!' They would have had them up again at Auckland Airport in 1970. New Zealanders will not admit failure and have no compassion for those who fail.

All the blame could not be put on Vodanovich, for there were several contributing factors, and one, perhaps, was the loss of Meads when playing well. Also there was the failure of the younger players to realise that test matches were very different from provincial matches, especially so in South Africa. Again, the Springboks just did not want to lose and some of their senior players were making their last appearances.

When England beat South Africa, surprisingly but deservedly, in 1971 at Ellis Park, South Africa were caught in between 'teams', since four regular and senior Springboks had retired, including three powerful forwards, and four regulars were injured. Yet this is the 'luck of the draw' and no country deserved more a change of fortune than England. The whole rugby world applauded the effort made. It was not good for the game that England should languish so long in the doldrums.

However in 1972, the New Zealand Rugby Union, always slow to change or cast aside a member of their body ... 'The Men in Black rarely feud in public or private, as do the Mafia, because they are all blood brothers' ... and so Vodanovich was re-elected chairman of selectors with Bob Duff, the big, quiet man from Canterbury, and Jackie Gleeson, a new national selector in place of Pat Walsh, who did not seek re-election. However, before the election, Vodanovich said he would not be available to visit the British Isles in 1972–73, so that the post of coach to the touring party was wide open again and the cause of much speculation in the land.

The New Zealand Union then announced that an All Blacks

side would make an internal tour, as the first step towards rehabilitation after failure in two seasons. Many of the old faces were discarded as the Meads Era ended, and Jackie Gleeson was made manager and coach of the side, which travelled round the two Islands playing excellent football and winning handsomely, while running with the ball. They even beat the Ranfurly Shield holders, North Auckland, at Whangarei, which was an achievement.

Several new All Blacks were blooded along the invincible home trail and Gleeson moved up to become a serious contender to Bob Duff as the coach for Britain. They were national selectors working together for the common cause, but rivals for the top job, and New Zealanders, as always, took sides in this domestic struggle! The establishment were for Duff, the senior man by Union standards, but the public were won over by the flair of Gleeson and his 'type' of open rugby. The Press, having toured with Gleeson, who treated them helpfully and with courtesy, moved away from Duff towards Gleeson. Chief candidate for the managership was tall Ernie Todd, a sound, long-serving N.Z.R.U. man from Wellington, who was hot favourite for the post in 1970, when he was pipped at the last moment by Ron Burke of Auckland. Then came the fateful day of appointment....

The manager was as anticipated – Ernie Todd, the Wellington business man with much experience of managing sides in New Zealand, who promised to do the job efficiently, and in a pleasant manner, as well as proving himself a diplomat and a good ambassador. I knew him well, and found him good company in N.Z. but still strong enough a personality to remain the boss, very much in charge of the side.

Those who have never had the job, or who have not lived close to tour managers, have no idea what a wearing and difficult task a long tour can be, even for the manager of a successful side – naturally, it is far worse when one is in charge of a losing side. If the reader is not convinced of this fact, please talk to those managers who have had to make speeches in defeat congratulating their opponents. It doesn't come easy when you are well aware that your players should have done better, or you should have had a better deal from the referee! How much I could say in praise of Alf Wilson, for his restraint after the 18–17 defeat in 1959, and in not saying what he must really have thought of N.Z. referees at the time.

The coach was the senior man; the Council's man; quiet, determined Bob Duff of Christchurch, an accountant by profession. He received preference over Jack Gleeson, as most people anticipated but one felt at the time that Gleeson's turn would come in the near future. Neither Todd nor Duff had been to the U.K. previously, but had seen a great deal of Lions' rugby since the War in New Zealand. They knew each other well and are both members of the N.Z.R.U. which makes them 'blood brothers'. As the corridors of rugby power in New Zealand are trod by few men, we appreciated that these two officials would be very much in step!

After his nomination, which pleased him immensely, Manager Todd said: 'The winning of the tests, and not the manner in which the other tour matches are played and won, will decide the success of the tour.

'New Zealand rugby has gone through an awkward transitional period but with the Colts tour, the internal tour and the Australian visit to N.Z., I will be surprised if the All Blacks' team does not develop into a very powerful side in Britain.'

Coach Duff commented: 'It is obvious that British rugby is better organised than it was, and with more coaching they will be a much tougher proposition than they've ever been.'

The Australian tour in N.Z. was completed without the All Blacks being really tested and all three tests were won comfortably at 29–6, 30–17 and 38–3. Barry John was there to watch the later matches and he commented, perhaps rather optimistically, at the end of the third and final test: 'From a British point of view, the day was just great... If this is the best by New Zealand, we in Britain are going to have a very happy few months!'

Then followed the New Zealand trials and, finally, on September 23, the names of the 30 players were announced and the list was full of surprises. Ian Kirkpatrick was rightly nominated as captain but several 'old hands' were omitted and instead, newcomers given their chance. Only seven members of the team that played in the last test against the Lions in 1971 were included, as the selectors executed a clean sweep. Apparently the team did not meet with the immediate approval of those present at Athletic Park and some were ready to call it the worst-ever side. At least, that was the headling above

Terry McLean's report on the selection in the *N.Z. Herald* on Monday morning. However, Terry always likes to add a touch of drama to his writing.

THE TEAM

Full-Backs

T. J. Morris (Nelson Bays), aged 30, weight 12 st. 7 lb., height 5 ft. 10½ in.; occupation, teacher; J. F. Karam (Wellington), 21, 12 st. 8 lb., 5 ft. 10 in., salesman.

Wings

G. B. Batty (Wellington), 20, 11 st., 5 ft. 5 in., insurance agent; G. R. Skudder (Waikato), 24, 12 st. 9 lb., 5 ft. 10½ in., teacher; D. A. Hales (Canterbury), 24, 13 st., 5 ft. 10 in., student (agriculture); B. G. Williams (Auckland), 21, 13 st. 8 lb., 5 ft. 10 in., student (law).

Centres

B. J. Robertson (Counties), 20, 13 st. 3 lb., 6 ft. ½ in., student (physical education); I. A. Hurst (Canterbury), 21, 13 st., 5 ft. 11 in., student (agriculture).

Five-Eights

R. M. Parkinson (Poverty Bay), 23, 12 st. 7 lb., 5 ft. 11 in., freezing worker; M. Sayers (Wellington), 24, 12 st. 7 lb., 5 ft. 11½ in., teacher; I. N. Stevens (Wellington), 24, 12 st. 3 lb., 5 ft. 9 in., clerk; R. E. Burgess (Manawatu), 23, 11 st. 9 lb., 5 ft. 10 in., student (botany).

Half-Backs

S. M. Going (North Auckland), 27, 12 st. 2 lb., 5 ft. 1½ in., farmer; G. L. Colling (Otago), 25, 11 st., 5 ft. 9 in., company representative.

Number Eights

B. E. Holmes (North Auckland), 26, 15 st., 6 ft. 2½ in., teacher; A. R. Sutherland (Marlborough), 23, 17 st., 6 ft. 3 in., farmer.

FLANKERS

I. A. Kirkpatrick (Poverty Bay), 25, 16 st. 2 lb., 6 ft. 3 in., farmer; A. L. Scown (Taranaki), 23, 15 st. 4 lb., 6 ft. 1 in., farmer; A. J. Wyllie (Canterbury), 27, 16 st., 6 ft. 1 in., farmer; K. W. Stewart (Southland), 19, 14 st., 6 ft. 1 in. (farmer).

LOCKS

A. M. Haden (Auckland), 22, 17st. 8 lb., 6 ft. 6½ in., student (science); P. J. Whiting (Auckland), 28, 16 st. 11 lb., 6 ft. 6 in., teacher; H. H. MacDonald (Canterbury), 24, 15 st. 10 lb., 6 ft. 3½ in., farmer; I. A. Eliason (Taranaki), 26 16 st., 6 ft. 3 in., farmer.

PROPS

K. A. Murdoch (Otago), 27, 16 st. 4 lb., 6 ft., farmer; G. J. Whiting (King Country), 23, 17 st. 9 lb., 6 ft. 3½ in., insurance agent; J. D. Matheson (Otago), 24, 15 st. 7 lb., 5 ft. 11½ in., farmer; K. K. Lambert (Manawatu), 20, 16 st., 5 ft. 10 in., student (agriculture).

HOOKERS

R. W. Norton (Canterbury), 29, 13 st. 4 lb., 5 ft. 11 in., bank officer; R. A. Urlich (Auckland), 28, 14 st. 6 lb., 6 ft., draughtsman.

The players were kitted out and prepared for the tour at Auckland, and stayed at the Royal International Hotel, from which hostelry the Lions left for their happy voyage home in August, 1971. The All Blacks flew into Vancouver and played British Columbia, achieving a comfortable victory by 31 points to three, after leading 11–3 at the interval. However, B.C. played with courage and Terry McLean spotted 'flaws' in the N.Z. approach which he highlighted in his report to Auckland.

On to New York for a match against the New York All Stars and, at half time, the All Blacks led by no more than 10–3, and six of the 10 were the result of a converted penalty try! In the end, the tourists scored 41 points, but were not always happy at the decisions of the referee, David Dyer, a former Australian – but then they have always been spoiled in New Zealand by having their own referees. Two players were injured, flanker Ken Stewart, with a badly torn ear, and full-back Trevor Morris, with a torn calf muscle, and they did not appear in the early matches in Britain.

The All Blacks had a night out in New York and then flew to London, reaching Heathrow Airport just before 10 p.m. to receive a V.I.P. welcome. Representatives of all four Home Unions were there, as well as a large Press Gang and a battery of cameras. They were tired, but in good spirits, and manager Ernie Todd, coach Bob Duff and captain Ian Kirkpatrick revealed diplomatic patience in dealing with questions from the Press while moving from the airport to their waiting coaches.

This was appreciated and I was able to phone a good 'read' through to the *Western Mail* for Monday morning, as readers were thirsting for information about the Men in Black. Even those popular dailes that do not claim to 'cover' rugby football were represented, and eager to report the arrival of the biggest, broadest, fastest, etc. This was good, as the Game – an amateur one – can never receive too much free publicity as it becomes more popular throughout the world.

Cliff Morgan drove me back to town where we took wine with the N.Z. Press at the team's hotel, and it was as if the memorable 1971 tour had never ended. In that pleasant hour, friendships were renewed and stories exchanged, but oh! – the price of the drinks was well in excess of the Royal International Hotel at Auckland, causing one Kiwi Pressman to comment with a sigh, 'We won't make much on expenses on this tour!' He didn't, but he enjoyed himself.

On Monday morning the management held its first Press conference and passed through the ordeal successfully, answering the questions, good and bad alike, in a friendly manner. There was enough copy available to make a reasonable story and everyone enjoyed the honest comment of Manager Todd when he said, 'I am a bad loser!' Unfortunately, he did not have to wait long to be a loser – it happened in the second match – but outwardly he accepted it with a smile and good grace.

Next followed a spectacular Lunch at the Savoy as the guests of the British Sportsmen Club, which was thoroughly enjoyed by all and, as a club member, I cannot recall a more illustrious gathering of famous rugby names. However, the Club's chairman, the Duke of Norfolk, received the loudest cheer when welcoming the tourists as he told them, 'The word "politics" will never be used where we (the Club) are concerned.'

The team had its first training session in Britain during the afternoon and enjoyed it. On Tuesday they trained again and were entertained by the Rugby Writers' Club. On Wednesday the N.Z. High Commissioner welcomed them and Thursday saw them leave London for Cheltenham in preparation for their first match against the Western Counties. The tour had started . . . there was excitement in the air!

4 *A Tough Start–Victory, Defeat and a Brawl*

We set off for Cheltenham on Friday afternoon and found the Motorways M4 and M5 speeded the process of travel considerably, enabling us to make contact before dinner with the management. There, too, was genial Ted Howard, the manager's secretary, as well as experienced R.F.U. liaison officer, Stanley Couchman, who has had this honorary duty for several tours and, with Handel Rogers of Wales, knows all the answers concerning the manners and habits of rugby tourists. Ted Howard is the brother of 1938 British Lion W. G. Howard, who appeared in a Test but never played for England.

Completing the touring party was pleasant Graham Shaw, the baggage master and general factotum, who was always most helpful to everyone. That made a party of thirty-five, plus seven pressmen, to be transported round the British Isles, a task organised as usual by T. H. Hamer and Company, of London. The team travelled in one coach and the press in another, this being standard procedure at home and abroad, although I recall with some delight the ready humour and amusing antics on the 1955 and 1959 Lions tours, when management, players and press travelled together. In those days, there were only two British pressmen travelling with the teams throughout the whole of the tours, and they did not report the private off-the-field activities of the party! However, as British press representation has increased – resulting in greater coverage and publicity for the game – there has ceased to be room on coaches or in 'planes for the whole 'show', and so the press party now has a coach of its own.

The seven-strong N.Z. press party (five writers and two photographers) had coaches of various sizes to convey them round the British Isles, although Bob Irvine and Terry McLean opted out occasionally when offered a lift by car. British writers have often done this in New Zealand and South Africa, as a car ride, generally, is quicker and more comfortable. One does, however, see a great deal more of the countryside by coach. Abroad, most of the travel is by air and one only sees the high mountains unless the weather is clear!

Cliff Morgan and I had a friendly drink with Ernie Todd and Bob Duff, and discussed prospects while looking out across the beautiful vista of the lovely town of Cheltenham. At dinner, Vivian Jenkins, Peter West and Janet of B.B.C. 2, joined my wife Gwen, Cliff and myself, but Cliff, on doctor's orders, retired to bed early. It was sad not to have him through the evening with his ready wit and mimicry, and his good sense when talking about rugby football. After two happy trips with Vivian and Cliff in 1968 and 1971, following the deeds of the Lions, one hoped that his recovery from a particularly serious illness would be speedy and complete. Truly one of the greatest of outside halves, Morgan would have been an outstanding and attractive performer in any era.

On Saturday morning the All Blacks decided to leave Sid Going out of the side, but when several people sympathised with him he seemed somewhat uncommunicative. The impression created was perhaps unfortunate and not quite what one has come to expect from an experienced tourist.

We set off for Gloucester at 11.30 a.m. and parked the cars outside Kingsholm before taking lunch and chatting across the tables of a Spanish restaurant to the England selectors and their party. There is always excitement in the air at the start of a long tour and the first day at Gloucester was no exception. The weather was ideal, the crowd enthusiastic, and the press box bursting at the seams. Eventually the teams fielded and it was action stations for the Seventh All Blacks.

Third Match (but first in Great Britain)

Versus Western Counties at Kingsholm, Gloucester, October 28.

New Zealand won by four goals, one penalty and three tries (39) to one goal and two penalty goals (12).

Weather: Fine. *Ground:* Good. *Crowd:* 16,000.

TEAMS:

WESTERN COUNTIES: P. Butler (*Gloucester*); A. J. Morley (*Bristol*), J. A. Bayliss (*Gloucester*), C. J. Williams (*Bristol*), P. M. Knight (*Bristol*); J. R. Gabitass (*Bristol*), J. A. Cannon

(*Clifton*); R. F. Cowling (*Gloucester*), J. V. Pullin (*Bristol*), M. A. Burton (*Gloucester*), D. E. J. Watt (*Bristol,* capt.), A. Brinn (*Gloucester*), J. A. Watkins (*Gloucester*), R. C. Hannaford (*Bristol*), R. Smith (*Gloucester*).
NEW ZEALAND: J. F. Karam; B. G. Williams, B. J. Robertson, R. M. Parkinson, G. B. Batty; R. E. Burgess, G. L. Colling; J. D. Matheson, R. A. Urlich, K. Murdoch, H. H. Macdonald, P. J. Whiting, A. I. Scown, A. R. Sutherland, I. A. Kirkpatrick (capt.).
Referee: D. P. d'Arcy (Ireland).

The Western Counties fielded an all-Gloucestershire XV with eight internationals, as a tribute to the County Champions of 1971–72 and in the hope that their team-work of the previous season would help combat the anticipated strength of the tourists. However, as the Western Counties were originally intended to be a side representative of both Gloucestershire and Somerset, the selection, quite naturally, did not please everyone. However, most English writers, including the provocative Terry O'Connor, believed it to be 'a wise decision because it means the New Zealanders will meet a team in every sense'.

To meet this threat the All Blacks fielded what they believed, at the time, to be near enough their strongest XV, apart from the late withdrawal of Sid Going with a torn ankle. Actually, his absence did not affect the outcome of the match, since deputy Lyn Colling played extremely well. An experienced player, who did a noble job as captain of Otago against the 1971 Lions, he sent out a long and accurate service to keep Burgess fully occupied at first five-eighth!

The match was a sell-out, all 16,000 tickets being taken up, readily, weeks before the day of the game. The interest was considerable, not only in Gloucester, Stroud, Bristol and Bath, but all over Europe. Pressmen poured in from many different parts, and all were accommodated. For this hospitality the Counties were deserving of praise. When the teams fielded there was an exciting air of expectancy, but really the match was New Zealand's from start to finish, except for a brief period in the second half.

Many critics had believed that the Counties would do well, but the side disappointed both themselves and their supporters, never revealing their best form. The All Blacks, in winning handsomely, also flattered a little to deceive most of the senior critics present, including myself. We thought after this first match that they were better than they really were, and blessed with a more friendly and open spirit on the field. Indeed, on the Saturday night, as we returned home, we pondered upon the possibility of a highly successful and attractive tour. We were pleased at this, as the challenge went out from the tourists – 'We are here; we will run with the ball, and we will win!' Even in Llanelli and Cardiff, doubts were expressed as to whether they could be beaten.

Welsh selector Cliff Jones told me, 'They are good, especially in the back row of the scrum, but they will be beaten!' Derek Morgan, coach to the Gwent XV, commented, 'You have got to contain their forwards, but which sides have eight forwards big enough to do so?' Carwyn James, who had to attend a wedding and missed the match, said, prophetically, in the mould of 'Witchdoctor' Smith, 'Despite the impressive start of the tourists, the Llanelli players are in great heart and I still believe we will do well!' The genial Chairman of the England selectors, Sandy Sanders, a most enthusiastic and likeable person, told me before he left Kingsholm, 'It was an impressive performance. We will have to work hard in England to match it, especially their forward domination.'

The Sunday papers gave the All Blacks full praise for their efforts, as Vivian Jenkins in the *Sunday Times* wrote: 'Rugby men of Britain, you have been warned! Forget the complacency after the victories of the 1971 Lions ...' Clem Thomas's report in *The Observer* was headed, 'All Blacks are so beautiful,' and he, too, warned British sides and related that the tourists had 'imposed immediately a massive dominance through their gargantuan pack'.

Wilfred Wooller who, like Jenkins and Thomas, had played in winning Welsh teams against previous All Blacks' sides, was also impressed. 'The All Blacks' side has all the shape of a very good team,' he wrote. Only one critic, the observant David Frost, in *The Guardian,* handed out a warning to the All Blacks, as if he was looking into his crystal ball. The heading on his Monday morning piece read, 'All Blacks must look to discipline'. How right he was in his forecast, for we did not have to wait very long to see the other side of the 'coin'.

However, in this match the All Blacks put on an excellent

showing and gathered confidence and momentum as the match proceeded. They played attractively and convincingly, succeeding as their illustrious predecessors had done in 1905, by beating the Champion County handsomely. The tourists had great power in front, except perhaps in the front row, where Burton, Pullin and Cowling did well for the Counties; dominated the line-out, particularly at the end, where Kirkpatrick, Sutherland and Scown at 6, 7 and 8 had matters, sometimes illegally, all their own way.

The combined drive of these three players and the support they and their backs provided, was the highlight of the performance. Nothing could stop their foraging, which set up several scoring situations, while Colling, at their heels, fed Burgess with an excellent service. The outside half, or first five-eighth, had a field day with such a regular supply of the ball and, against a back row committed to close defence, he was able to run freely and cut out openings in the Best British style, rather than kick in New Zealand style!

Obviously, the drill on how to contain them was simple enough, provided future sides had the ability, power and pace. The scrummaging was straightforward, but at the line-out there had to be a contest, with each opponent standing up to each All Black, jumping wih him and blocking any breakthrough. Again, referees would have to prevent them getting off-side at the end of the line-out, and also blow up for obstruction.

Every ruck would have to be contested, the All Blacks' drive met with an equal drive, and there would have to be accurate rib-shaking tackling. Every All Black in possession would have to be put to ground, and the play had to be carried to them. No side could afford to wait for the All Blacks to come to them, as the tourists had to be harassed and turned. Yet these obvious tactical plans were to disturb the tourist as they became extremely upset if held or 'turned', and their press took strong objection to anyone employing All Blacks methods against them, as we were to discover, yet again, very early in their tour. Their press motto, as always, was 'The All Blacks can do no wrong,' and their reactions were sad, because whatever one writes for 'home' consumption, it always finds its way back to the host country. The more one-sided the comment, the more likely it is to be sent back to the U.K. by the N.Z.P.A. from Wellington.

The All Blacks took the lead against the Counties with a penalty by Karam and then came three tries before the interval by Parkinson, Robertson and Parkinson again, and all three were converted by Karam, an accurate place kicker on the day and a sound full-back, though he was never really tested as Gabitass kicked badly for the Counties from the outside half position.

In the second half, Colling scored a try and then Williams, running really well, scored a hat-trick of tries, one of which Karam converted. In reply, Burton got a good try from a short penalty which Butler, a promising full-back, converted for the Counties, as well as kicking two penalty goals, to make the final score 39–12 in favour of the tourists. Yet neither management nor captain was satisfied, saying, 'We can do better!'

The hors d'oeuvres were over and enjoyed and now eyes were turned to the main course, at Llanelli, being prepared with Celtic relish by chef internationale, Carwyn James, in his traditional sospan with plenty of scarlet sauce! As the All Blacks moved into Wales on the Sunday and took up headquarters at the Dragon Hotel, Swansea, they were decidedly apprehensive. They were young and inexperienced in the overseas touring atmosphere, and especially the Welsh atmosphere which, for better or worse, is unique in the game.

While the tourists were travelling by coach from Cheltenham to Swansea, I was breaking my arm (fortunately, my left one) just above the wrist while walking with Gwen in Llandaff Fields, a pleasant spot between the Cathedral and my home. There followed a loud crack after I had slipped on the wet autumn leaves, but the staff of St David's Hospital did an excellent job and, after a spell in the operating theatre, they put the matter right. However, this meant the arm being in plaster for five or six weeks – and the tour just starting!

I cursed myself for being so awkward and faced up to the problem of not being able to drive a car or use a typewriter – two vital factors in covering a tour. However, the handicap was eased considerably by the help of friends, especially two members of my loyal staff, Jill Mathias and John Billot, without whose ready and cheerful aid this book would not have been completed!

The pain was not the worry, but the inconvenience, although I quickly learned to dress and shave myself one-handed. It was having to write everything in longhand and then have this typed out that caused the frustration. This accident, following a leg injury received in September, which was still being treated, meant that I could expect to be a patient at the Newport clinic of that excellent masseur, Gerry Lewis, for many months! As my friends told me, old age never comes alone, not even to rugby writers! I would certainly have much more sympathy now with players injured on the All Blacks' tour, whatever the colour of their jersey! Regularly, I had telephone consultations with Gordon Rowley, of Swansea, and he cheered me no end with his optimism and sound medical advice.

On Sunday evening the All Blacks announced their side for the Llanelli game; it showed five changes from the team that defeated the Counties, but Trevor Morris, Sid Going and Skudder were still not fit, while Tane Norton, chosen as hooker, had to withdraw before the kick off. Llanelli were at full strength, with pivot man Phil Bennett reporting fit, although the playing of Gareth Jenkins on the flank was regarded as a something of a gamble, as he had been injured for some time.

The *Western Mail* published an eight page supplement launching the tour but this was apparently regarded by some members of the N.Z. press gang as a 'war of words'. Terry McLean complained in *The Times,* under the pseudonym of Harold Power, while Bob Irvine, of N.Z.B.C., who should have known better, said such things never happened in New Zealand! All this made me laugh, and amused Carwyn James even more. Indeed, in all my association with the game I have never known an All Blacks side as fearful of one man, as they were of college lecturer, Carwyn James. His reputation, clearly established in 1971 in their country, made him the Rugby Enemy No. 1 of all New Zealanders – a Welsh Merlin, master of rugby tactics.

James, a brilliant thinker and speaker on the game, gave numerous interviews before the match, and wrote a special article on the All Blacks' strengths and weaknesses in the *Western Mail* supplement and, I believe, this disturbed them a little. The tourists were feeling their way and to meet Llanelli, coached by James and captained by Delme Thomas, who had three times visited New Zealand, plus the fact that five members of the club side had played in N.Z. and one other member visited the country, was a tall order. The fixture list with three

The Tour Management: (*Left to right*) S. M. Going (vice capt.), I. A. Kirkpatrick (capt.), H. Rogers (Welsh liaison officer), E. L. Todd (manager), and R. H. Duff (coach)

Glyn Turner, the Gwent scrum half, dives over to score one of the tour's most spectacular tries, in the last minutes of the match

Delme Thomas, the Welsh captain, starts the movement that led to the disallowed try by John Williams – it's action all the way!

such hard initial matches should not have been accepted, for the Lions would not like Canterbury, Auckland and Otago as their first three! However, the seventh All Blacks had to face the music, but even they did not anticipate such a reception, such crowd enthusiasm, such tremendous and inspired opposition as experienced at Stradey Park on October 31, 1972.

There were such traffic jams on the main roads leading to Llanelli some hours before the match, that the tourists had to be accompanied from Swansea to Llanelli by police cars and outriders, with klaxon horns screaming. John Billot drove me down and we left Cardiff at 11 a.m. but only arrived at Stradey Park at 2.30 p.m. The ground was full – all programmes sold – there was singing and marching bands, and one sensed victory in the air!

Officials chatted, and I wished the referee, Mike Titcombe, a good match (which indeed he had – quite his best in Wales), because he always seems to have tough matches in which Welshmen appear. There was all-consuming tension and excitement abroad, and one expected Carwyn James, albeit out of context, perhaps, to quote the famous lines from Shakespeare's 'Henry V', in the manner of Sir Lawrence Olivier with a delightful, musical Welsh accent.

While there was hustle and bustle in and around the ground, as last minute spectators hurried into position, it was the traditionally cool, calm and collected Delme Thomas who was putting the necessary 'Sospan fire' into the nervous but receptive bellies of his team. Thomas, a most likeable, unspoiled, sincere rugby man, appealed to his team thus . . .

'I have been round the world and gained all the honours possible, but I would willingly give them all away if only you will win this match for me. Our mothers, wives and girl friends are sitting in the stand watching us today, and if you want to do something for me, as well as them, it is to beat these All Blacks. Don't let me down!'

Some of the team cried with the emotion, but Thomas, with his honest simplicity in words, had set the fuse. Fifteen men in scarlet jerseys felt eight feet tall and they were going to die for Delme and their club!

The All Blacks had to sit in their dressing-room listening to the singing, and when they took the field there was five minutes more of singing and marching. The Scarlets soaked in the atmosphere and the sense of urgency while the All Blacks, quite naturally, became more apprehensive, for Stradey Park seemed no normal rugby ground!

Fourth Match
Versus Llanelli at Stradey Park, October 31.
Llanelli won by one goal, one penalty (9) to one penalty (3).
Weather: Dull and damp. *Ground:* Soft. *Crowd:* 23,800.
TEAMS:
LLANELLI: R. Davies; A. Hill, R. T. Bergiers, R. Gravelle, J. J. Williams; P. Bennett, R. Hopkins; A. Crocker, R. Thomas, D. B. Llewelyn, W. D. Thomas (capt.), D. Quinnell, T. David, H. Jenkins, G. Jenkins.
NEW ZEALAND: T. J. F. Karam; B. G. Williams, B. J. Robertson, M. Sayers, D. A. Hales; R. E. Burgess, G. L. Colling; K. Murdoch, R. A. Urlich, G. J. Whiting, A. M. Haden, P. J. Whiting, I. A. Kirkpatrick (capt.), A. R. Sutherland, A. I. Scown. *Replacement:* G. B. Batty for Williams.
Referee: M. H. Titcombe (England).

I had waited long, as indeed had many Welshmen, to read my old friend Terry McLean acknowledge that an All Blacks team had been fairly and squarely beaten in Wales. At long last the pleasure was enjoyed and even old 'Crusty' himself, as Gabe David calls him in happy moments, had his *N.Z. Herald* report of the match headed – 'All Blacks out-thought, out fought – Magnificent play by Llanelli', and he went on to write, 'the better team by a long margin, won the game.'

Llanelli achieved their greatest hour in the game, and in their Centenary Year, to join the elite group of clubs, all Welsh, who have conquered the N.Z. tourists – Cardiff, Newport and Swansea – and this was a prize that had eluded them since 1888. Proud, partisan, volatile, generous and wildly ecstatic, yet intensely loyal, the good folk of Llanelli – a town not 40,000 strong – had every reason to celebrate and if, as reported, the pubs ran dry by 8 p.m., a little over three hours after the match had ended, it came as no surprise to someone like myself, who has visited the classic slopes of Stradey Park since the late 1920's. It was a day to remember!

Not even Albert Jenkins, Ivor Jones and the many great idols of Stradey Park had been able to overcome the All Blacks, and down through the years the desire to succeed had become an obsession, albeit a healthy one, and the scarlet jerseyed knights of the Stradey Round Table had girded their loins in search of the Holy Grail of Rugby Football. Perhaps the Golden Fleece would be more apposite but their King Arthur was Delme Thomas, and their Merlin, Carwyn James; and their real strength was in their cause, their eagerness to succeed and bring honour to the club in its centenary year.

All that had gone before, the hours of practice, coaching lecturing and encouraging (in the same manner as did the Wellington team before beating the Lions in 1966 and the Waikato team in beating the Springboks in 1956), produced the elusive and now treasured result – victory – convincing and deserved. The *Western Mail* carried the headline 'Good Old Sospan Fach!' and never before had the Club's symbol boiled over with such unrequited joy – indeed, words cannot fully express the joy and satisfaction of the hour for Llanelli.

The British Press went mad – they had to – since every representative there was overwhelmed by the emotional, happy atmosphere. The hands of several quaked a little as they wrote their reports, for even the hardest of critics could not but feel elated and moved, by what they had witnessed on the classic slopes of Stradey Park.

The headlines the next day made interesting reading, while the sales of the *Western Mail* increased by nearly 20 per cent, thanks to the victory, the exciting play and the Town's enthusiasm for the game. "Shattering', said the *Daily Express;* 'Llanelli master All Blacks at their own game' – *Daily Telegraph*; 'The match of the Llanelli Century' – *The Times*; 'All Blacks humbled' – *Daily Mirror*; 'Llanelli among the immortals' – *Daily Mail*; 'All Blacks founder on Llanelli' – *The Guardian*; and away in New Zealand, the *Sunday Times* of Wellington said, 'Welsh sting All Blacks,' and this headed a telephone interview with Manager Ernie Todd.

Llanelli were in the headlines – on top of the rugby world – and had shown the way to overcome the tourists. Coach Carwyn James, rejected by the Welsh clubs and the W.R.U. executive, had been completely vindicated – what he could do abroad with the best thirty players in the British Isles he could also do with his club side. Surely, now, all would acclaim him as a master of applied rugby tactics – or did he deserve a doctorate?

He had argued, before the All Blacks arrived in London, that they could be beaten if their loose forwards and scrum-half, Sid Going, could be held in check. That's what he had planned for Llanelli, and to ensure at all times that the play would be carried to the All Blacks' territory. Going was not fit enough to play in this match and, while he was missed, I do not think he would have made any real difference to the result. On the day, the All Blacks were well and truly beaten – out-thought and out-fought!

As Carwyn James told me soon after the end of the match, 'All fifteen Llanelli players were heroes,' since no player played less than above himself from first whistle to last. However, it was the pack of eight forwards who really gave everything in a hard battle of physical contact. Delme Thomas was superb, rising to the occasion as a leader like Lloyd George in war-time, but with a coolness and sincerity not always associated with that political leader! Derek Quinnell was just about the best forward on the field, working equally hard in the tight and the loose, and was the strong man that New Zealand could not subdue. He was the complete answer to any play, good or bad, rough or clean, and his smile throughout must have annoyed the tourists!

The All Blacks lost this match because they could not get enough good ball; for once, they were put under continual pressure and found wanting. They were inflexible and had no alternative plan or tactics, preferring to battle it out at forward in the hope that Llanelli would crack, but the home side refused to yield. As the match progressed, Llanelli's grip became tighter, and the crowd, almost beside itself with rapture at the thought of victory, guided them home.

Llanelli set a cracking pace from the first whistle and took play to their opponents' line to score within three minutes. A kick at penalty goal by Bennett from 45 yards rebounded from an upright for Colling to field and attempt to clear to touch. Llanelli's young Welsh centre, Roy Bergiers, was up to charge down the kick and fall on the ball for a try, as it shot over the All Blacks' line. Bennett kicked a good conversion and Llanelli were six precious points in the lead and never to be overhauled in a further 80 minutes of dramatic, hectic, exciting and, sometimes, skilful play.

Joe Karam, who proved a very brave full-back, kicked a

penalty goal after 25 minutes and the match was balanced perilously until the 31st minute of the second half, when Andy Hill landed the most important penalty goal of his colourful career as a kicker from 50 yards. The ground erupted, for New Zealand had to score twice to win, but only once in the closing 10 minutes did they get near to it, and then Bennett, who had played in masterly fashion throughout the match, cleared from his own corner-flag with substitute Batty round his neck, by as narrow and perfect a line kick as he will ever produce. When the final whistle went the field was engulfed, and Delme Thomas was carried shoulder high from the field in triumph. The Llanelli dressing-room was a circus – that of the All Blacks a morgue, with heads buried in hands. It had been an emotional experience for everyone – even for Referee Mike Titcombe, who did an excellent job in keeping the steaming cauldron from boiling over!

Terry McLean, again writing under the pen name of Harold Power, in *The Times,* of all papers, condemned Titcombe for being 'abrasive and personal'. It was the first of many press squeals that were to follow – as always, New Zealanders are never wrong in rugby. They were shaken by the defeat, far more than their management revealed but, on arrival in Cardiff the next day, both Manager Todd and Captain Kirkpatrick said the team had got over it. Coach Bob Duff told New Zealand: 'Defeat can only do us good. Now that the All Blacks have seen for themselves what Welsh rugby is, they will understand the realities. Llanelli were a good side. They were as well drilled as I have seen. They knew exactly what they had to do and did it consistently and well. Now we must come back to developing the same sort of aggressive attitude in the All Blacks!' They did, as the next match at Cardiff was to prove. Although we had expected a hard match there, what we did witness was a disgrace to New Zealand and Cardiff, a disservice to Rugby Football.

Yet before that match was to take place at the National Stadium, the Cardiff Arms Park, there was plenty of activity. The All Blacks trained at B. P. Llandarcy on Wednesday morning before travelling to Cardiff in the afternoon and visiting Pontypool Park in the evening to watch Gwent playing the London Counties in a fog. They left at half time, no better off, for like the two groups of county selectors they had seen nothing!

On Thursday they trained at the University College Ground at Llanrumney and Bob Duff, quite wisely, concentrated on the line-out play. There was still doubt over the fitness of Trevor Morris, Tane Norton and Sid Going, but only Morris eventually had to withdraw and was not to play in the next four matches. Fortunately, Joe Karam, if uncertain with his place kicking, was to play extremely well in the absence of Morris, but the need for a replacement full-back was drawing near.

On Thursday evening the whole touring party were entertained by the Deputy Lord Mayor of Cardiff at the Castle in the spectacular Banqueting Hall. On Friday evening, the management and non-playing members were guests at the reunion of the 1953 Cardiff side that defeated Bob Stuart's All Blacks. The Deputy High Commissioner for New Zealand attended, together with many other rugby V.I.P.'s and the night (indeed, early morning) was a roaring success, mainly due to Chairman Hubert 'Mao' Johnson, Stanley 'Admiral' Bowes and Billy 'The Coal' Cleaver, plus Bleddyn 'Skipper' Williams and his committee. It cost £10 a shot – the dearest rugby dinner in history – but it was worth it. Rothmans were represented and gave away a copy of their Rugby annual and cigarettes to each guest. Yet, if this was the true spirit of rugby, all were to get a rude awakening the next day, when we witnessed, not a match of quality but a brawl – totally unnecessary – with the blame equally apportioned and deserved by both teams, the referee, and a large section of the crowd!

Fifth Match
Versus Cardiff at Cardiff Arms Park National Stadium, November 4.
New Zealand won by one goal, two penalty goals and two tries (20) to one try (4).
Weather: Damp and windy. *Ground:* Good. *Crowd:* 46,000.
TEAMS:
CARDIFF: J. Davies; W. Lewis, N. Williams, A. Finlayson, J. C. Bevan; K. M. James, G. O. Edwards; M. Knill, G. Davies, R. Beard, I. Robinson, L. Baxter, R. Lane, C. Smith, M. John (capt.).

NEW ZEALAND: J. F. Karam; B. G. Williams, B. J. Robertson, M. Sayers, G. B. Batty; R. E. Burgess, S. M. Going; J. D. Matheson, R. W. Norton, K. Murdoch, H. H. Macdonald, P. J. Whiting, A. J. Wyllie, B. Holmes, I. A. Kirkpatrick (capt.). *Replacement:* G. J. Whiting for Matheson.
Referee: J. Young (Scotland).

The All Blacks had to win, come what may, because they had never previously suffered two successive defeats in the British Isles. Cardiff wanted to emulate Llanelli and thus the match threatened to be a confrontation, just as physical as Llanelli, with the All Blacks, as promised, putting a lot more into it. Cardiff said they would seek to contain the All Blacks forwards and the All Blacks said they would drive and drive in search of victory!

The day was perfect for rugby and 46,000 spectators were in the National Stadium, one of the world's most historic grounds. The referee was Jake Young, of Scotland, who had had an excellent France v. Wales match in 1971, but one felt he was unprepared and surprised, in all probability, by the conduct of the match he had to control. Neither side seemed to want to play sporting rugby, preferring to get at one another, and he, as the referee, was too kind. He hoped they would improve with encouragement, but what they needed was the 'big stick'.

Mr Young is a friend, but in this match he appeared the reluctant referee, for had he sent players off from *both* sides he would have been a hero. The situation required it, though distasteful; one has sympathy for him in his predicament, but players who continually break the law with over-vigorous play must be sent off. Down through the years our best referees have leaned over backwards to avoid sending players off in touring team matches.

Those that have done so, have not been praised but criticised, but I admire them and after the Cardiff match I felt that, eventually, on the tour someone would have to go, unless things improved. A cable was sent back to New Zealand saying there was a 'campaign' to get an All Black sent off. What nonsense this was – emphasising their belief that a New Zealander can do no wrong! In this match the two teams were at one another the start – it matters little who lit the fuse because the intent was already there – victory at any price.

Even after this short lapse of time I can recall little that happened in the match in the rugby sense, but plenty of brawling – disgusting fighting, punching, wrestling and fouling, such as the karate chop upon Gareth Edwards after he scored his try and the left hook that K.O'd prop Jeff Matheson. Both acts were ungracious and disturbing, and while there was plenty of provocation given by both sides, one vital maxim was not maintained.

A touring team in any land must behave itself – come what may – on the field. It must accept referees' decisions and not 'ask' continually. The Lions of 1971 showed the way in this and one felt the All Blacks of 1972 were unduly petulant and impatient, and this may have been due to inexperience. If Cardiff lost friends, the All Blacks certainly gained no new ones, and disappointed to such an extent as to find themselves booed and slow handclapped by a crowd that previously held a world-wide reputation for sportsmanship and the appreciation of good rugby. This match tarnished, in some degree, that reputation.

To see groups of players wrestling and punching some 40 yards from the ball, was a rugby nightmare in a match of this importance, and then to have the referee say at the end of the match, 'I did not warn any player,' was a complete surprise. I can only say that several referees I know would have 'gone among the warring players' like the village constable of old and quelled the rioting.

The All Blacks well deserved to win the match, such as it was, for they were the better of two brawling sides. They had the superior forward drive, won more possession and gave the elusive, determined, individualist Going a ready supply of the ball. The scoring matters little, but in the first half, Joe Karam kicked two penalties and Ian Kirkpatrick got a good try, while Cardiff wasted chances. In the second half, Mark Sayers and Bob Burgess scored tries, one of which Karam converted. Gareth Edwards scored a good unconverted try for Cardiff.

The function after the match was friendly, but away at their hotel, several members of the N.Z. press were 'composing' their reports, which were all mailed back to me within five days, by a very faithful Auckland friend. I was amazed at some of the comments, but am glad to say that British writers condemned both sides, and the match, out of hand. It truly was a disgrace.

The headlines were bold and meaningful and *The Scotsman* headed my report, 'Mean, moody and very unmemorable rugby.' Quite true, while Barry John, an expert in beating the All Blacks but new to the Press Box, commented, 'The All Blacks are glad to see the last of Wales for the time being'.

The days that followed saw many an article published in New Zealand and Britain demanding this and that but, most of all, improved conduct by the players and stricter refereeing. The cries of 'It was them, not us,' could be safely ignored, for the game had to be protected as it was still more important than the tour, New Zealand or the Cardiff Club. It was a salutary warning to all concerned, but 'trampling' by New Zealand and 'jersey pulling' by Welshmen had to be eradicated. Another match like this would not rock but sink the boat!

5 *England and Ireland*

The All Blacks left Cardiff on Sunday for the cultural warmth of Cambridge. No doubt they were much relieved to leave the land of the Dragons and the Merlins, where there are rugby players just as hard as themselves, coaches just as clever as their own, and followers who are just as 'one-eyed' as those in New Zealand, but with a far greater sense of humour – or so it has always seemed to me!

New Zealand as a nation – proud, loyal and sincere – takes its rugby far too seriously, and this is in contrast to Wales where the Welsh can switch the 'devotion' off and laugh at themselves. The New Zealand press, if they be representative of their nation, and I am not altogether certain that they are so, enjoy emphasising the difficulties, the struts and frets, the set backs, the minor injustices, and rarely, if ever seem to laugh, at least in their writings. One feels they are almost afraid to allow their personal humour to show through in what they write.

Only one, Gabe David of Wellington, used to laugh in his writings, although Terry McLean's personality comes through, vividly at times, in his articles, and one feels that he is still with the N.Z. Division in Italy, of which he was an honourable member. In contrast British critics, for all their alleged 'technical' weaknesses as far as the game is concerned, can laugh in their writings, even if they are at times given to what is known throughout the world as 'the Fleet Street touch of sensationalism'. Perhaps this is not entirely the fault of the writers themselves but of those who are the unseen 'persuaders', the re-write men.

Again, there are far more amusing stories about the game in Wales than in New Zealand, and no New Zealander would have dared to emulate Michael Green with his 'Coarse Rugby' although one leading cartoonist, Neville Lodge, has done his best to bring a smile to the 'Unsmiling Giants'. I have never seen an All Black smile on the field of play – or perhaps I did, once!

It was Don Clarke, one of New Zealand's greatest match winners, when he scored the vital try at Wellington in 1959, in the closing minutes of the Second Test, and robbed the Lions of certain victory. He allowed himself a half smile, as well he should have done, for had the Lions won that match they would deservedly have shared the test series.

The N.Z. Press, though personal friends of mine, take their rugby far too seriously. For instance, Roy Williams of the Auckland *Eight O'Clock* Saturday evening sports paper, previewed the tour with the heading, *Wipe the Smiles off their dials, Kirky*. After the Cardiff match, members of the travelling Press cabled home, *Rugby is War in Wales!*

The cables flowed back to New Zealand from Cardiff on the Saturday night after the match, and from Cambridge on the Sunday, their heated words almost blistering the keys of the teleprinters in the G.P.O.'s mobile cable coach, not to mention the keys of the receiving machines in Wellington, the initial N.Z. receiving station! Soon the powerful pieces of prose were being relayed back to London, only short excerpts of course, but five days later my faithful contact in New Zealand had supplied me with the full reports.

Talk about the 'wicked' scribes of Fleet Street; they appeared as just beginners in the art of 'stirring' in comparison with some members of the N.Z. travelling press, who had accused the Welsh papers of launching a 'war of words'. How naïve can one be? Still, reading them provided amusement, and one was forced to appeal to them to stop their 'bickering' and get on with the tour. Both sides were 'at it' at Cardiff, so what good could be achieved by one side trying to blame the other?

It is much easier just to report what you see happening on the field of play rather than to base one's report on the reaction of players after the match. Unfortunately, the 'Quote' system is wide spread south of the Equator, but what if the Welsh press had reported all the 'quotes' of the Llanelli and Cardiff players after their matches! Such material would have ranked as a best seller! As for the N.Z. Press ACTUALLY to report that Referee Mike Titcombe had sworn at a New

Zealand flank forward and *put him off his game* – surely, they don't still believe in fairy tales?

But I must quote John Brooks of N.Z.P.A., on his first tour, when he cabled home . . . 'The All Blacks did Rugby Union a service in convincingly beating the punching, jersey-pulling, early-tackling Cardiff team.' If all that was true, and perhaps much of it was, does anyone honestly believe, as Mr. Brooks apparently did, that the All Blacks were guiltless? I ask only one question . . . 'Who karate chopped Gareth Edwards as he scored?' It was a case of the 'kettle calling the pot black' and it was the 'white washing' of the All Blacks by the N.Z. Press (while the British Press really castigated both sides) that was the sad result of a thoroughly disgusting match.

One could not help but attack both sides and the referee, and I suggested in the *Western Mail*. 'Referees must be brave . . . send off the rogues, or the tour may be a farce.' Then I pointed out: 'Violence on the rugby field is ugly, whichever players in whatever colour jerseys are guilty. If New Zealand trampling at the rucks, or Welsh jersey-pulling at the line-out, starts the trouble then referees must clamp down immediately. There is a deterrent against rough play, and if the penalty kick does not work, then it must be sending off. If this is neglected, players sense they can opt out of the law and remain on the field.' The game had to be protected from the 'villains'.

The 'woes' of the tour are discussed in detail elsewhere in this book and so it was pleasant to forget the Cardiff match and set off with Gwen for Cambridge by train, and not car, via Paddington and King's Cross, as must have touring teams in the 'good old days'. The trains may be faster nowadays, but not by any large margin, and they are certainly dirtier; even the first-class compartments would have appalled GWR inspectors between the Wars, and certainly before 1914, when every section was spotlessly clean and comfortable. The decline and fall of British Railways, as a result of losing a one-sided battle against the internal combustion engine, is one of the saddest features of the post-war era, and for me, I am with the Poet Laureate in his praise of the old G.W.R.!

I was also slightly 'foxed' by the King's Cross route to Cambridge, and the old Great Northern line from Hitchin to the city of learning with such stations as Baldock, Ashwell and

Royston. Yet to pull into Cambridge with its long single main platform, that used to serve three companies when railways and King Steam reigned supreme, was still a thrill. It is the atmosphere and character of the 'good old days' that is lacking in British Railways.

The All Blacks were installed at the University Arms, an excellent and confortable establishment, as Mr Pickwick would have said, with a good menu and wine cellar at reasonable prices. Yet the tourists were still quiet and in reflective mood, at least until 4 a.m., when some of the non-players engaged in a little 'horse play' which the hotel staff quickly repaired the next morning. Let no one ever believe the fairy story that no 'wreckers' ever came out of New Zealand and that only Lions damage property. I recall, too, what happened in the North British Hotel after the Scotland v. New Zealand match of 1967, when Meads was sent off – still, no names, no pack drill, for such things are common to ALL rugby touring teams. There are NO whiter than white teams, not even in All Black jerseys!

As always, like a good tourist, Ian Kirkpatrick shook hands and chatted for a moment but the vice captain was still uncommunicative.

A strange attitude compared with that of Charlie Oliver, of 1935, Laurie Haig, of 1953, and Kevin Briscoe, of 1963; not to mention the dignified and polite Jack Finlay, of the 1945 Kiwis. This was a purely personal impression, and I could have been wrong, but many notable British rugby men appeared to come to the same conclusion. On the field, of course, he was the best and most dangerous back in the side yet there is something more to a tour than merely playing football!

Wednesday morning was spent sightseeing in one of the most beautiful university towns in the world, while the 'dirt-trackers' played soccer on the historic Parker's Piece that ran alongside the hotel. Bob Duff joined in and it was good fun as the weather was perfect, like a July day on the high veld of South Africa or a June day in Christchurch, N.Z. Yet I wonder how many of the young All Blacks trying to master the art of soccer – a gimmick on rugby tours advanced by Barry 'King' John – realised it was on the greensward of Parker's Piece that one of the world's three greatest batsmen, John Berry Hobbs, learned his craft before moving on to Surrey. On that sunny morning I wished that I could have watched again a magical hundred by that immaculate, unhurried, wristy, effortless stroke player, who shall for ever be remembered as the 'Master', not forgetting the other two knights of the green, Dr W. G. and Sir Donald. Cricket and Cambridge have a close affinity, though not as much nowadays, as the academic and the social scientist seem to frown on the sportsman.

Sixth Match
Versus Cambridge University at Cambridge, November 8.
New Zealand won by three goals and four tries (34) to one penalty goal (3).
Weather: Fine. *Ground:* Good. *Crowd:* 8,000.
TEAMS:
CAMBRIDGE UNIVERSITY: I. S. Williamson (*Sidcup G.S. and Fitzwilliam*); G. P. Phillips (*Cray Valley G.S. and Queen's*), J. M. Howard (*Birkenhead and Trinity*, capt.), N. W. Drummond (*Merchison and Fitzwilliam*), S. Page (*Haberdashers Askes and Emmanuel*); C. R. Williams (*Bridgend G.S. and Clare*), R. Harding (*Millfield and St John's*); G. Rees (*Neath G.S. and Emmanuel*), J. M. Smith (*Neath G.S. and Selwyn*), C. P. Goodall (*Sherborne and St Catherine's*), D. R. Thomas (*Llandeilo G.S. and Christ's*), R. M. Wilkinson (*St. Alban's and Emmanuel*), A. D. Foley (*Fettes and Christ's*), J. P. Dickins (*Oundle and Corpus Christi*), W. A. Jones (*Campbell College, Belfast and Queen's*). *Replacements:* T. Lintott (*Blundell's and Christ's*) for Goodall; A. Walker (*Luton G.S. and Emmanuel*) for Williamson.
NEW ZEALAND: J. F. Karam; G. B. Batty, I. A. Hurst, R. M. Parkinson, D. A. Hales; I. N. Stevens, S. M. Going (capt.); K. K. Lambert, R. A. Urlich, G. J. Whiting, I. A. Eliason, A. M. Haden, A. J. Wyllie, A. R. Sutherland, K. W. Stewart. *Replacement:* A. I. Scown for Sutherland.
Referee: G. Domercq (France).

The undergraduates put on a good show and although in the end they were comfortably beaten by seven tries and three conversions to a penalty goal, their spirit never wavered. For most of the play they had only 14 men on the field, as players left for attention or to be replaced, and after two replacements had been drafted into service the injured had to carry on as best they could. Yet it was not a dirty game, although often vigorous with an occasional 'climb in', and the French referee, Georges Domercq, did quite well, to suggest that he would be looked upon with favour if elevated to the International panel.

However, it was a case of brave young men, not long out of school, meeting an international side. The British Lions had played Oxford University last season under the flimsy 'guise' of Major Stanley's XV, and won by a big margin, so no one expected Cambridge to do more than keep the score down to reasonable proportions. In the circumstances their effort was a worthy one and they did have the best forward on the field in Bob Wilkinson, the 21-year-old lock, who gave the more experienced tourists a lesson in two-handed catching at the line-out.

Well though the All Blacks played at times – and right-wing Grant Batty was the star with four excellent tries – there were moments of stupidity which brought criticism from the crowd. They 'climbed in' feet first at many a maul and, once, a forward jumped on the back of an opponent lying unprotected at the side of a ruck. In fairness to Terry McLean, he emphasised this in his dispatch to the *N.Z. Herald,* while I could not resist turning round in the Press Box and commenting, 'They're at it again!' Such an act is never clever in any match, by any player of any country, and completely out of place in a match of this nature, where the result, really, was a foregone conclusion.

After he had suggested there was a campaign abroad in Britain to get an All Black sent off during the tour, McLean realised the men in black could be naughty and cabled home: 'But criticism should surely come from within when players commit such foolish acts in such an unthinking manner as to arouse resentment and invite retaliation or, worse, the pain and embarrassment of an ordering off.' Thus it was confirmed that the All Blacks were not blameless, as John Brooks and others had suggested after the Cardiff match. They were human after all!

It took the All Blacks some time to come to terms with their opponents who tackled with determination and cleared their line with last-minute touch-finders. Wilkinson denied them the ball at the line-out for a long time and it was 25 minutes before the tourists registered their first score, a try by Batty, and only one more followed by the same player before the interval. Thus the undergraduates could feel well pleased with their first 40 minutes of brave defence since they did not produce any great skill in attack, in which their favourite ploy was the kick ahead.

However, after the interval it was a different story, and with injuries being suffered at regular intervals there was little chance of any continuity in the Cambridge approach. Going started running from the set pieces and, although careless at times with his passing to Stevens, a player considerably lacking in experience of the outside half, or first five-eighth, position, the scrum-half was always a menace. Again, if the overlap was not created for Batty, then the diminutive Wellington wing generally managed to beat his opposite number!

It would be fair to suggest that had Going and Stevens combined more smoothly, and Stevens set his backs moving more readily, plus more accurate place kicking from the continually improving Joe Karam at full-back, the All Blacks' tally could have reached the half century. Gone are the days when Oxbridge could field sides strong enough to threaten a touring team, even though Oxford defeated the Springboks in the 'demo' match of 1969 at Twickenham. This state of affairs has been arrived at for many reasons and is a sad one, as University life which should represent at the highest level all the skills of man, both in the lecture room and on the playing fields. However, my opponents of this 'square' belief may point out that the 1935 All Blacks, though just beating Oxford by a mere point at 10–9, crushed Cambridge by 25–5 with Cliff Jones, Wilfred Wooller and Ken Fyfe in the back division. Poor John Howard, the 1972 Cambridge captain, and son of a 1938 Lion, was disappointed at the result, but there was nothing more he could have done to reduce the margin of defeat. He and his side suffered from the shortcomings of contemporary sport at Oxbridge.

In addition to Batty's four tries, two more came from an active No. 8 Alan Sutherland, and one from the stern flanker, Alex Wyllie. Three of the tries were converted by Going (2) and Karam (one), but Karam failed with four conversions, three penalties and a drop at goal. John Howard kicked a penalty goal for Cambridge University.

Peter Whiting, the No.2 lock, raises his arms in triumph as Referee Johnson awards the Keith Murdoch try against Wales. Barry Llewelyn (No.3) tries to indicate to the referee that Murdoch was tackled short of the line (*Below*): referee Johnson disallows the 'try' by John Williams, and starts another 'Deans' controversy. The Welsh players at least have no doubts!

Keith Murdoch, the 17 stone prop, who was sent home after the tour's most serious incident

In the fog: Sid Going draws in Doug Schick before sending out the pass to Duncan Hales from which the latter scored the All Blacks first try against East Glamorgan

After the match the All Blacks held a singing session in their 'allocated' bar at the University Arms before going to the after-match dinner, and Gwen and myself had a pleasant dinner at the Royal Cambridge Hotel with friends, who knew much more about the city than most guide books.

Before we set off for London and home in the morning, we saw the All Blacks move off for a training session. Both Bob Duff and Ian Kirkpatrick admitted there was still work to be done and later in the day they announced their side for the first appearance at Twickenham, against the London Counties on the Saturday. It was a good side and near enough to their Test XV, apart from one or two players who were injured.

At this stage, they were particularly worried about full-back Trevor Morris although Karam was doing a wonderful job in his place, while Skudder was still troubled by his hamstring injury. The London Counties represented reasonable opposition, if nothing like as strong as it could have been, had all the London Welsh club's Lions been available. Such players as John Williams, Gerald Davies, Jeff Young, Geoffrey Evans, Mike Roberts and John Taylor would have made a considerable difference.

John Dawes, the 1971 Lions' captain, coached the side and actually played in the match despite a nasty eye injury sustained seven days previously; the former England captain, Tony Bucknall, of Richmond, led the side. On paper it appeared to lack the necessary hardness in front and enough cohesive skill at half-back and three-quarter, and so it proved on the day. The fact that the date clashed with the Welsh trial was a blow to the London Counties and to those players involved who could have had two bites of the cherry against the touring All Blacks, making their presence felt by their experience and, particularly their knowledge of the New Zealand players and approach.

Seventh Match
Versus London Counties at Twickenham, November 11.
New Zealand won by two goals and three tries (24) to one penalty goal (3).
Weather: Fine. *Ground:* Good. *Crowd:* 30,000.
TEAMS:
LONDON COUNTIES: A. M. Jorden (*Blackheath*); A. Richards (*London Welsh*), S. J. Dawes (*London Welsh*),

D. A. Cooke (*Harlequins*), M. P. Bulpitt (*Blackheath*); C. D. Saville (*Blackheath*), W. G. Hullin (*London Counties*); R. L. Barlow (*Rosslyn Park*), A. V. Boddy (*Metropolitan Police*), R. L. Challis (*London Scottish*), C. W. Ralston (*Richmond*), M. G. Molloy (*London Irish*), A. L. Bucknall (*Richmond*, capt.), A. G. Ripley (*Rosslyn Park*), S. James (*London Welsh*).

NEW ZEALAND: J. F. Karam; B. G. Williams, I. A. Hurst, R. M. Parkinson, G. B. Batty; R. E. Burgess, S. M. Going; J. D. Matheson, R. W. Norton, K. Murdoch, H. H. Macdonald, P. J. Whiting, K. W. Stewart, A. R. Sutherland, I. A. Kirkpatrick (capt.). *Replacement:* M. Sayers for Hurst. *Referee:* G. A. Jamieson (Ireland).

After this match, David Frost wrote a most interesting analysis in *The Guardian* headed 'All Blacks not yet able to match their predecessors'. Later I wondered whether he had borrowed Dr Douglas Smith's crystal ball, particularly in view of the result at Workington! John Reason produced the best report of the match in the *Daily Telegraph*, but Terry McLean's headline in the *N.Z. Herald* was bold enough to suggest, 'All Blacks just short of greatness in their victory'. This contrasted with Reason's headline, 'Two dubious tries help All Blacks master London'. While reporters are not responsible for the headlines put above their stories, these are, of course, based on the content of the reports.

The London side was too loose at the rucks and failed to launch any penetrative attacks mainly because Billy Hullin and Chris Saville, at half-back, did not have a happy day. However, the All Blacks did not really justify McLean's headline, for even Ian Kirkpatrick was not happy about his side's performance, although he was full of praise for Referee Jamieson, of Ireland. In my view, however, two of the All Blacks tries should not have been allowed, even though they thoroughly deserved to win. Of course victors and vanquished alike are never responsible for refereeing errors and, often, at ground level referees do not see obvious errors which can be easily detected from the upper reaches of the stands, especially at a major ground like Twickenham.

One important error occurred when a penalty award was made to the All Blacks and Referee Jamieson waved the touch judges to the posts. Thus it was understood that Karam, as the kicker, had indicated his intention of kicking for goal. Then Karam, seeing that a number of London players were assisting Saville from the field with a cut head, took a short tap-penalty instead of placing the ball, re-gathered it and raced over for a 'gift' try, but in so doing he dropped the ball over the line. Referee Jamieson should have ordered a scrum and not given a try.

In the second half a further error occurred which presented another score to the All Blacks. Sutherland threw forward as he was tackled; the tourists won the ruck and Burgess kicked to the open side, where Bryan Williams awaited the kick in an off-side position. He went on to score and Karam converted it. Again, at many a line-out with London to throw in, the Tourists were allowed to extend it, while they barged at the four-men line-outs without being penalised. No wonder the All Blacks praised Mr Jamieson!

Yet his errors of omission did not really affect the result, even if the final margin flattered the All Blacks, because the All Blacks scored one of their best tries of the tour, which was repeated several times on B.B.C. TV, and recalled for older viewers the tourists' glorious days of the past.

London shoved hard at a scrum to lift the All Blacks' front-row, but the ball went back to Going and, as in the Second Test of 1971 at Christchurch, the opposing back-row forwards remained down with the shove, even though the ball was lost! Going spotted this quickly and shot away on the blind side before a London back row forward raised his head. He moved away into the open field to link up with his own back-row. Kirkpatrick took the pass and set in motion a glorious 75 yard movement which ended with Ian Hurst selling a dummy and scoring on the left, after Stewart, McDonald, Burgess and Parkinson had handled. A good try this, but it was one of the few occasions for the All Blacks to really sparkle in the match.

In the end the All Blacks won by three goals and two tries to a penalty goal, and their tries were scored by Sutherland, Karam, Hurst, Williams and Batty with Karam converting two. Jorden kicked a goal for the London Counties, who did not have the power or ability to contain the Tourists who, themselves, were never really in top gear. Yet they had won the first match of the tour at Twickenham, as they had done at the Cardiff Arms Park, but one felt that against the best of opposition they would be vulnerable.

While in London, two important things happened to the tourists: they visited Buckingham Palace to be received by the Queen, and it was decided to play the match at Belfast against Ulster. Their visit to the Palace was much enjoyed and both the Queen and Princess Anne discussed horses with the tourists. The Ulster Rugby Union were overjoyed with the decision and laid on special security precautions to ensure the smooth conduct of the match in a city suffering what was virtually the agony of a civil war. The N.Z.R.U. told Manager Todd and his team that they should go, and it was a bold decision, fully justified by a successful match.

But first the All Blacks had to visit Dublin and face quite strong opposition from Leinster, while they suddenly changed their minds and decided to stay at Porthcawl for a whole week, on their next visit to Wales, for the matches against Gwent and Wales and 'hide away'. Their excuse was that Test week would be too hectic in Cardiff and they would be 'much better off at Porthcawl'. All previous teams had complained about having to be shut off from things at the seaside town in winter. The question was asked, 'Were the All Blacks becoming anti-social?'

When the tourists reached Dublin, Terry McLean did some heart-searching and cabled back to New Zealand what many Britishers had been thinking for some time, but about which they had been too polite to speak or write – that the All Blacks lacked humour, discipline and courtesy. With amazing honesty, he revealed that John Dawes had complained about the All Blacks 'trampling', and that the Lions' captain had commented: 'I was stamped by All Blacks forwards during the match. I did not care for that!'

What was happening to the side? What was at fault at this stage? Was it a lack of skill, experience, training, managerial discipline, or some 'chip upon the shoulder?' Were they sensitive or suffering from an inferiority complex in the company of British officials and VIP's? Were they really too young for the job? Did the side lack the necessary percentage of senior players? Had the management failed to develop them or understand them, or did they fail to respond? Many questions passed through the minds of British critics at this stage of the tour, but most worrying was the tourists' apparent lack of humour, their excessive tenseness and the fact that they did not appear to enjoy their rugby.

Ireland afforded the All Blacks a great welcome and among those who 'shook the hand' of the visitors were Karl Mullen, Ronnie Dawson, Ray McLoughlin and Wig Mulcahy, all fine Irish forwards who had served various Lions' sides exceedingly well in New Zealand. Off the field, the Irish are as gracious as they are rumbustious on it; yet all without malice. When Irishmen play rugby they pretend they 'hate' the enemy, but in the heat of the 'battle' they can always laugh, even at themselves, and this endears Irish rugby men to opponents everywhere.

Leinster, the first Irish opponents, had selected a good side, headed by that most genuine and lovable of prop forwards, Sean Lynch, as captain. During the Maori match at Auckland in 1971, an opponent clouted Lynch across the face and caused him to retire for the insertion of stitches, but the Maori retired shortly afterwards with a broken arm! With Lynch were Duggan, Flynn, Grace, Maloney, and the singer of Irish ballards par excellence, Fergus Slattery, a more than useful flanker!

Eighth Match
Versus Leinster at Lansdowne Road, Dublin, November 15.
New Zealand won by a goal, a penalty goal and two tries (17) to a goal and a penalty goal (9).
Weather: Dry. *Ground:* Firm. *Crowd:* 20,000.
TEAMS:
LEINSTER: A. H. Ensor (*Wanderers*); T. Grace (*St Mary's*), K. Flynn (*Wanderers*), P. Andreucetti (*St Mary's*), A. T. A. Duggan (*Lansdowne*); M. Quinn (*Lansdowne*), J. Moloney (*St Mary's*); S. Lynch (*St Mary's,* capt.), D. Barry (*Wanderers*), N. Dwyer (*UCD*), C. Feighery (*UCD*), K. Mays (*UCD*), J. Craig (*Lansdowne*), F. Slattery (*Blackrock*), W. Duggan (*Blackrock*). *Replacement:* P. Inglis (*Lansdowne*) for Slattery.
NEW ZEALAND: S. M. Going (capt.); B. G. Williams, M. Sayers, D. A. Hales, G. R. Skudder; I. N. Stevens, G. L. Colling; G. J. Whiting, R. A. Urlich, K. K. Lambert, P. J. Whiting, I. M. Eliason, A. J. Wyllie, A. I. Scown, B. Holmes.
Referee: M. Joseph (Wales).

There was a firm belief held by British and Irish rugby

writers that the All Blacks would do well to survive against Leinster at Lansdowne Road, as their spirit and determination, (call it Celtic fire) would disturb the tourists. Referee Meirion Joseph was in charge of the match, and the first

Welshman to officiate on the tour, as well as completing an interesting hat-trick, having 'blown' in the previous tours of 1963 and 1967.

He experienced no trouble, and it was an exciting match, only for Leinster to 'give it away' in the closing stages and, again, it was the 'luck of the Irish' that let the All Blacks in for a last minute victory. I did not see these first two maches in Ireland because my arm in plaster was not conducive to travelling and dashing about, but TV filled a need, and I was able to watch much that was interesting in the continuation of this narrative. It is true that the TV recordings are edited, but one gets the feel of the match, if 'black patches' are often omitted!

Leinster were leading by nine points to seven with 10 minutes left for play, and looked capable of holding out. Lynch and his pack were thinking, 'We can make it. We can become the first Irish side ever to defeat the All Blacks!' Then disaster struck! Scrum-half Lyn Colling shot away to the open side from his own '25' and belted the ball downfield, where the two wings Duggan and Grace, went to gather. They got tangled up and put George Skudder over for a try and it was 11–9.

This try broke the back and spirit of the brave Leinster side and it mattered not that the All Blacks scored again, when full-back Ensor dropped a high punt from Sid Going, playing in the same position, and Peter Whiting was up to gather and charge over for a try that Going converted. So it was 17–9, a score that did not reflect the play or the respective merits of the two sides, but for the record it was 17–9. Previously, in the first 70 minutes, Bryan Williams kicked a penalty goal and Wyllie scored a try for the tourists, while Willie Duggan collected a try for Leinster which Ensor converted as well as kicking a penalty goal.

On the Thursday afternoon the All Blacks party moved quietly to a secret hide out, twenty miles from the centre of Belfast, at Dunadry, in a pleasant country hotel which seemed to please every one and was far enough way from the scene of the unfortunate troubles which have plagued Ulster for so long and robbed it of its share of representative rugby. No little wonder that members of the Ulster Rugby Union, protestants and catholics alike, were delighted to welcome the tourists. The warmth of the welcome was much warmer than the weather!

Ulster had gathered a good side together but, unfortunately, the peerless star of the province, the superb all-round midfield player and probably the greatest support player of his generation, Michael Gibson, could not play. He had aggravated an old injury in his back while playing for the Cambridge Past and Present XV in the University's Centenary Match against the Barbarians and it had not come right in time. This loss was impossible to make good, however well the side played, for Gibson had been the star of the Scottish Union's Centenary Match at Murrayfield and wanted to play against the All Blacks on his own midden, since he had done so much with Willie John McBride to bring home the 'bacon' from New Zealand in 1971.

At the time, one only hoped that his back would improve for him to make the Irish side in the New Year. I believe that many of the All Blacks party especially the Press men, were sad not to have the privilege of meeting him on the field. Still Ulster had a good side and Ken Kennedy and McBride, with their considerable experience of New Zealand rugby, promised to stiffen a pack that was capable of testing an All Blacks side that included six test players.

Ninth Match
Versus Ulster at Ravenhill Park, Belfast, November 18.
New Zealand won by one goal, three penalty goals and a try (19) to one goal (6).
Weather: Cold and wet. *Ground:* Soft and slippery. *Crowd:* 18,000.
TEAMS:
ULSTER: B. D. E. Marshall (*CIYMS*); J. Myles (*Malone*), R. A. Milliken (*Bangor*), A. Goodrich (*Queen's*), H. McKibbin (*Instonians*); A. Harrison (*Collegians*), W. R. Oakes (*Instonians*); P. J. Agnew (*CIYMS*), K. W. Kennedy (*London Irish*), R. J. Clegg (*Bangor*), W. J. McBride (*Ballymena*, capt.), C. W. Murtagh (*Portadown*), J. C. Davidson (*Dungannon*), S. A. McKinney (*Dungannon*), H. W. Steele (*Queen's*).

NEW ZEALAND: J. F. Karam; B. G. Williams, M. Sayers, D. A. Hales, G. B. Batty; R. E. Burgess, S. M. Going; J. D. Matheson, R. A. Urlich, K. Murdoch, A. M. Haden, H. H. McDonald, I. A. Kirkpatrick (capt.), K. W. Stewart, A. J. Wyllie. *Replacement:* G. W. Skudder for Williams.
Referee: R. F. Johnson (England).

Strict security precautions had been taken at the famous Ravenhill Park ground which resembled an Army stronghold on Saturday morning, but one could never be sure, as the three N.Z. official photographers found when they entered the city. Two of them were seriously interrogated for taking pictures.

The ground was ringed by armed soldiers ready for action, but the roar of the large crowd of over twenty thousand enthusiasts, thirsting for the good old rugby days, was proof enough that the All Blacks, by agreeing to fulfil the fixture, had brought a touch of sanity back to a scene of tragic conflict, and a little warmth and relaxation to hearts and minds to those living often in fear and terror of the next bomb outrage. The crowd contained protestants and catholics, who should always live together in peace, and because they were rugger folk, I like to think that they could do just that.

It pleased one man immensely, Harry McKibbin, the 1938 Lion, chairman of Ulster Union and a member of the International Board, who had worked so hard to keep contact, across the water, for rugby football to be played at Dublin and Belfast... 'You cannot imagine what this has really meant to all of us connected with rugby in Ireland, and especially Ulster, but until the All Blacks took the field we couldn't just believe the match was on. We will always be grateful to the Seventh All Blacks.

It was not a pleasant day for good rugby, with a cold wind and rain and Ulster, like grateful hosts, made too many mistakes behind the scrum to give themselves a chance of winning. Their forwards played superbly but their backs, without the guiding hand of Gibson, lacked accuracy and confidence while the All Blacks in spasms, did well. Yet their one attacking player, normally above average in midfield, Burgess, kicked continuously instead of moving his line, even against the excellent tackling of the Ulster backs and the covering of the back row. Even Going found it difficult to make progress, and I noticed on the TV recording a certain leniency on the part of an otherwise splendid referee, Johnny Johnson, to allow the All Blacks back-row to slip the ball, in the drive, to colleagues slightly ahead of the ball carrier.

Perhaps, the most important weakness of the day was the scrummaging of the All Blacks, against McBride forming a hard Ulster core in the 'Meads' manner. More leniency on the part of Referee Johnson in allowing Going to put the ball into scrum, plus the fact that the All Blacks put the ball in twice as frequently as Ulster, hid this basic weakness. Towards the end of the second half, McBride achieved his ambition by getting the Ulster pack really to drive and produce a try.

Once again Bryan Williams had to leave the field, after 65 minutes, with ankle trouble and was replaced by Skudder, but it was a case of Ulster missing their chances and the All Blacks taking theirs. Always, they are better at pouncing upon opposing errors for scores, rather than creating their own and they exert pressure to force errors. It is their standard pattern of play and, of course, there is the added value of accurate place kicking. Burgess got an easy try after charging down a clearing kick and Hales got a good try after Going had run across the defence. Karam converted the Burgess try and kicked three penalties, to collect another valuable eleven points for his side. Steele, a fine back-row forward got Ulster's try and Marshall, a brave full-back, converted beautifully.

British critics present in Belfast were not impressed by the All Blacks showing and praised Ulster, while Peter West quoted the Ulster coach, Maurice Crabbe, in *The Times* as saying, 'The tourists are certainly beatable. For all their greater size, they can be matched up front, physically.' Yet Bob Howitt, deputising for me in the *Western Mail* in his own attractive style, argued that the All Blacks have a theory about British rugby: 'They have become so obsessed with scrummaging and defensive patterns that they have forgotten how to score points.' As a gazer into the mythical rugby crystal ball, Mr Crabbe was the more accurate for, at Workington, in the very next match, the All Blacks were to lose and their opponents registered more points that the seven previous British sides!

6 *Defeat and Precious Victory*

New Zealanders generally might have heard of Workington before this tour, but did not realise or worry why the town existed. However, after the visit of the Seventh All Blacks to the small industrial town on the coast of Cumberland with 28,414 inhabitants, all New Zealand awoke one morning to realise that Workington could be renamed Waterloo. The first touring team to visit the ground – the first victory by a provincial side over a N.Z. side in England, and a sharp reminder that English rugby was no longer going backwards!

The All Blacks moved from Belfast to Keswick and immediately set about improving their scrummaging by practising hard there. It was reported that the players 'riled' each other on the training field, and they were still not a truly friendly side. They had not learnt how to become ambassadors, and one heard rumours to the effect that certain members of the team were 'running' the side rather than the management!

The North Western Counties team had been announced over a week before the match from a squad following a practice match against the East Midlands during the previous week. John Burgess, the volatile coach, called a former Carlisle player, Chris Wardlow, now of Coventry, back to the side and this was a masterstroke, for Wardlow was to prove himself one of several Workington heroes, although later he was to announce that he did not wish to be considered for the England team!

The side included six international players in addition to Wardlow, with Fran Cotton, a developing prop forward, being named as captain. It looked a good side on paper, with Steve Smith as the most promising inside-half in England but, best of all, it was expertly coached by John Burgess, who had taken an England team to the Far East and then been dropped for John Elders. Strange things happen to officials in all countries, and Burgess was keen to prove himself as good as the next man in the art of coaching.

Terry O'Connor, in the *Daily Mail*, quoted three top coaches, John Burgess, Maurice Crabbe and Carwyn James, as saying that the legend of the All Blacks' invincibility was all in the mind. Burgess appeared to have no doubt at all that they could be beaten. As the All Blacks included only seven of these who were to play against Wales in the following week, it could be called the Wednesday team, but the cheering news was the inclusion of Trevor Morris at full-back. Everyone hoped he would do well, since there is nothing worse for a player on tour than having to sit in the stand, match after match, unable to play.

The All Blacks stayed at Keswick in the lovely Lake District, but it was the rainy period as the lakes were being topped up, something like the Monday after the first Test of 1971, when the Lions revived themselves at Queenstown! Rain keeps a touring side indoors, generally; not that the 1972 All Blacks needed much encouragement to do so. The Northern's flanker, Tony Neary, waited until the morning of the match to declare his fitness.

Tenth Match
Versus North West Counties at Workington, November 22.
North West Counties won by a goal, one dropped goal, one penalty and a try (16) to two tries and two penalty goals (14).
Weather: Squally. *Ground:* Reasonable. *Crowd:* 12,000.
TEAMS:
NORTH WEST COUNTIES: B. J. O'Driscoll (*Manchester*); A. A. Richards (*Fylde*), C. S. Wardlow (*Coventry*), D. Roughley (*Liverpool*), S. Maxwell (*Richmond*); A. R. Cowman (*Coventry*), S. Smith (*Sale*); F. E. Cotton (*Loughborough Colleges,* capt.); J. Lansbury (*Sale*), W. F. Anderson (*Orrell*), R. Trickey (*Sale*), M. Leadbetter (*Broughton Park*), D. Robinson (*Gosforth*), A. Neary (*Broughton Park*), P. J. Dixon (*Gosforth*).
NEW ZEALAND: T. J. Morris; G. R. Skudder, D. A. Hales, M. Sayers, G. B. Batty; R. E. Burgess, G. L. Colling; G. J. Whiting, R. A. Urlich, K. K. Lambert, I. A. Eliason, A. M. Haden, I. A. Kirkpatrick (capt.), B. E. Holmes, A. R. Sutherland. *Replacement:* S. M. Going for Colling.
Referee: T. F. E. Grierson (Scotland).

The North West Counties made rugby history in the grand manner by becoming the first English provincial side to defeat the All Blacks in 67 years of trying. They thoroughly deserved their cherished moment of glory. Fran Cotton was carried from the ground shoulder high; he, with his 14 colleagues, had played their hearts out for John Burgess and England, and what a reception the folk of Workington, better used to Rugby League than Union, gave them and what a blow was struck for the Union cause in the North West. So much, too, for the passing over of Burgess . . . this was his real hour . . . and there to congratulate him at the end of the match, among many others, were Carwyn James, the scourge of the All Blacks, and John Elders who took over the England team. They were both full of praise for Burgess and critical of the All Blacks.

It was a hard match – most matches against touring teams are – but there was only one flurry of punches, involving All Black lock Haden who swung at Leadbetter, his opposite number, and followed by Lambert, the young All Blacks prop who apparently had a 'blackout' and swung punches at everyone. The incident lasted only for a couple of seconds and Referee Grierson soon had the game under control and no one was disturbed unduly.

Yet throughout, the Northerners – with Cotton, Smith and Wardlow outstanding – revealed more persistence and flair. Considering this was the work of a combined side as compared with an established and historical club like Llanelli, it was a famous victory. Perhaps, the All Blacks were stronger at Llanelli where they had to contend with an emotional atmosphere, yet one would regard the Workington victory as equal in effect. It did a power of good for English rugby and set the All Blacks thinking that nowhere in these Islands could they afford to relax. In as many words, it was good for them. In the other countries too there was rejoicing, for the victory indicated that the England team's win in Johannesburg in the Summer was no isolated fluke, and that the old spirit of the 1920's, when Englishmen were respected and feared on all grounds, was fast returning.

The result of a goal, a dropped goal, a penalty and a try to two tries and two penalties, producing a 16–14 finish, was the climax to a see-saw contest. The Counties' players stuck to their Burgess plan courageously, and not only held the All Blacks but forced them into errors. They did even better at the rucks and mauls and, as David Irvine wrote in *The Guardian,* outwitted the All Blacks on a tactical level. The tackling was first class and, more important perhaps, the North West also ran with the ball and made very few mistakes. There were few crumbs for the All Blacks to collect from the table and they, in turn, were forced into many more errors.

Best work for the North West was done not so much at the line-out but what followed, and the clever work of Smith at scrum-half, quite the best performance in the position against the All Blacks up to that time, and one of the best of the tour. Cowman was steady at outside-half and Wardlow was a tower of strength in the centre, and never mind the cliché! O'Driscoll at full-back caught almost everything and Maxwell got two tries on the left wing – the result of clever running and handling.

There were two unusual incidents in the match. Lyn Colling, the All Blacks scrum-half, was injured and Sid Going was rushed on to the field since Colling's hand was badly lacerated. John Burgess objected and asked whether Going had received permission as Graham Short, the All Blacks team assistant, signalled Going to go on to the field. Short was disturbed by the action of Burgess and when the coach apologised, Short asked him to do so to the N.Z. management. After the match all was well.

The other, earlier incident concerned Grant Batty, on the wing. He attempted to delay a throw-in from a line-out while Colling, who had lost a boot, stopped to put it on again. Referee Grierson awarded a penalty and Cowman kicked a valuable goal.

After the match Mr. Todd, the N.Z. manager, reprimanded Lambert for punching, but he was a young player, only trying to copy what his seniors often did in other matches. Batty was told to 'get on with it' and forget about gamesmanship. Some New Zealanders argued that the winning try scored by the Counties was not a try, since the ball was thrown in to flank forward Neary who was not a part of the line-out. However he stood well back from a 'reduced' line-out, and could decide the length of the line-out because it was his own team's throw-in. The try was therefore 'in order'.

From Neary the ball was tapped down to Cotton who drove

through powerfully and fed Cowman. He made ground and sent a high pass to Wardlow who merely guided it on to to Maxwell who raced for the corner into glory. From 14–12 the score changed to 16–14 and the North West were home and dry!

Maxwell scored the two tries, Cowman converted one and kicked the penalty, while Wardlow dropped the goal for the North West. Batty and Skudder got tries for New Zealand and Morris kicked two penalties. At the interval the tourists led by 10–9. Motivation carried the day but there was also a touch of additional skill that was so important. Carwyn James and John Elders appeared on TV with Cliff Morgan after the match and praised both the team and Burgess. They were critical of some aspects of the N.Z. approach, although later James commented, 'Maybe they have not so far shaped like a vintage N.Z. side but, make no mistake, there is enough ability in their first fifteen for the All Blacks to improve greatly on what they have mostly shown so far.'

In this observation, James was wise and shrewd, and in the very next match, with a stronger side in the field, there was a considerable improvement. The Rest of the Scottish Districts were met at Hawick and easily defeated but the Scots played poorly until revived by two replacements in the closing stages.

The Scottish Districts appeared as an ill-chosen side, with the recall of Peter Stagg, the tallest lock in the game, unbalancing the pack. He and McHarg, although experienced internationals, were not ideally suited as a pair, while several of the pack had to be drafted in because of the non-availability of the leading Scottish forwards. Only two, Peter Brown and MacEwan, were truly members of the reigning Scottish pack. The New Zealanders rested Sutherland but twelve of the side were later to play against Wales, and Scown was to act as a replacement in that test.

Hawick is a wonderful rugby town, with a fine club side and a great tradition, but I do not think any of the 10,000 were overjoyed at the disappointing display of the Scots or happy at the excessive vigour of some of the All Blacks forwards.

Eleventh Match
Versus Rest of Scottish Districts at Hawick, November 25.
New Zealand won by two goals, two penalty goals and two

tries (26) to two penalty goals (6).
Weather: Dry. *Ground:* firm. *Crowd:* 10,000.

TEAMS:
REST OF SCOTTISH DISTRICTS: A. R. Brown (*Gala*); W. C. C. Steele (*Bedford*), J. N. M. Frame (*Gala*), J. M. Renwick (*Hawick*), L. G. Dick (*Loughborough Colleges*); I. R. McGeechan (*Headingley*), I. G. McCrae (*Gordonians*); N. Suddon (*Hawick*), F. A. L. Laidlaw (*Melrose*), R. D. H. Bryce (*Bristol*), A. F. McHarg (*London Scottish*), P. K. Stagg (*Sale*), N. A. MacEwan (*Gala*), P. C. Brown (*Gala*, capt.), W. Lauder (*Neath*). *Replacements:* D. Aitchison (*Highland*) for A. R. Brown, J. Henderson (*Melrose*) for McCrae.
NEW ZEALAND: J. F. Karam; B. G. Williams, R. M. Parkinson, D. A.Hales, G. R. Skudder; I. N. Stevens, S. M. Going; K. Murdoch, R. W. Norton, J. D. Matheson, H. H. McDonald, P. J. Whiting, I. A. Kirkpatrick (capt.), A. J. Wyllie, A. I. Scown.
Referee: J. Kelleher (Wales).

The Rest of Scotland gave such a poor display partly because the SRU did not encourage it to assemble before Saturday morning, assuming that all would be well 'on the day'. It was – for the All Blacks, who romped home! However, in the last twenty minutes one wondered who was winning, as the Rest suddenly found themselves, inspired by two young substitutes, David Aitchison at full-back for Arthur Brown, the international who unluckily suffered a fractured tibia, and Jim Henderson at scrum-half for Ian McCrea who cracked a breast bone.

However, it was too late then and the failure of the Scots to support the ball carrier and their obvious lack of tactical 'know-how' made it too easy for the All Blacks, who were extremely pleased with their win. For them the sight of Peter Stagg almost permanently standing at the front of the line-out trying to interfere with their throw-in from touch, was unbelievable!

The Rest of Scotland collected two early penalties by Peter Brown with his 'circus' like act as a successful place kicker, but then the All Blacks went ahead steadily and collected 26 points scored by Skudder, Hales, Going and Parkinson with tries and Joe Karam, the ever improving full-back and place kicker, who converted two and kicked two penalties.

Kirkpatrick liked the surface of Hawick's Manfield Park and the refereeing of Welshman, Jeff Kelleher of Wales, a new member of that Country's panel. The All Blacks regarded the Scots as the weakest team met on tour, up to that time, but even though their own play had improved on Workington, it was still not good enough. Kirkpatrick, generally, made this comment after a reasonable victory but obviously he was concerned with the final 20 minutes of play, and this fact was to worry him again at Ebbw Vale and even more so against Wales in the test. Would they become known as the fading All Blacks?

The All Blacks flew down from Scotland to Cardiff and went on to Porthcawl where they had gone 'for peace and quiet' during test week. Little did they realise, as they arrived at the Seabank Hotel, Porthcawl that they were on the brink of one of the most momentous periods in New Zealand touring history – not at Porthcawl, perhaps, but when they set off from the seaside town on Saturday morning, bound for Cardiff, to have lunch and play against Wales, a chain of events were set in motion which, when they ended, shocked the rugby world. More of this later, for first the All Blacks had to meet Gwent at Ebbw Vale.

Gwent comprised of a combined side selected from the Clubs of Monmouthshire, other than Newport who played as a separate club. It was led by international No. 8, Dennis Hughes, who had toured with Wales in New Zealand in 1969, and was coached by Derek Morgan, a Newbridge dental surgeon and former England No. 8. The Gwent side made no claim to greatness but it contained fifteen honest triers with good spirit and a determination to do well.

Ebbw Vale is a great-hearted town, a steel town, and I knew it well as a youth when it suffered its years of depression, and before the playing of this match the town again received bad news from the Steel Corporation, suggesting the possibility of unemployment. Yet the town is different in approach from Llanelli and, at this time in history, the rugby clubs of Gwent were not doing well. The most successful was Abertillery and they had no representative in the Gwent XV, which came as a surprise to all concerned. Ebbw Vale supplied five, Newbridge five and Pontypool three members of the side but it lacked the weight, height and pace of the All Blacks, who fielded a side that contained eight of the test XV to meet and beat Wales, in somewhat fortuitous circumstances, on the Saturday. But first to Ebbw Vale and the rain – the late November and early December plague of South Wales, from the central hills to the sea, for when it rains, it is most reluctant to stop!

Twelfth Match
Versus Gwent at Ebbw Vale, November 28.
New Zealand won by a goal, a penalty goal, a dropped goal and a try (16) to a penalty goal and a try (7).
Weather: Damp and showery. *Ground:* Soft. *Crowd:* 18,000
TEAMS:
GWENT: R. Pugh (*Pontypool*); A. Browning (*Newbridge*), I. Taylor (*Pontypool*), R. Duggan (*Bedwas*), R. Parry (*Ebbw Vale*); M. Grindle (*Ebbw Vale*), G. Turner (*Ebbw Vale*); A. Faulkner (*Pontypool*), A. Williams (*Newbridge*), G. Howls (*Ebbw Vale*), S. C. Geary (*Newbridge*), R. Bendall (*Newbridge*), G. Evans (*Ebbw Vale*), D. Hughes (*Newbridge, capt.*), T. Cobner (*Pontypool*). *Replacement:* A. Tucker (*Blaina*) for G. Evans.
NEW ZEALAND: T. J. Morris; G. R. Batty, R. M. Parkinson, M. Sayers, D. A. Hales; I. N. Stevens, S. M. Going; K. Murdoch, R. A. Urlich, G. J. Whiting, A. M. Haden, P. J. Whiting, K. Stewart, A. R. Sutherland, I. A. Kirkpatrick (capt.). *Replacement:* A. I. Scown for Batty.
Referee: K. Pattinson (England).

It suffices to say that Ebbw Vale welcomed the All Blacks and the Gwent XV gave them a hard game. The tourists won, as anticipated, but they made heavy weather of it, and had the Gwent XV been more venturesome and pursued victory by moving what little ball they had, the margin would have been much closer. The All Blacks won a lot of ball and set up attacking positions with good possession but were much too static behind. It was a wet day with a slippery ball but, even allowing for this handicap, they should have scored many more points.

Gwent tackled extremely well and covered bravely, while a strict referee, one of the best and fairest of the tour, Ken Pattinson of the North Midlands, a new member of the English panel, allowed no nonsense. He was tall and commanding and kept up with the play. He was the boss; the controller, and I felt he was just the answer to the Seventh All Blacks, because he would allow them nothing outside the laws.

To me he was the man of the match, although Glyn Turner's cheeky blind side try for Gwent in the closing stages, earned him a large number of marks, while Alan Sutherland made a big effort to ensure his test place at No. 8. At the end of a rather unattractive match, spoiled by the weather, Gwent's lack of real confidence until the last twenty minutes, and New Zealand's dullness behind, opinion was divided as to how well the All Blacks would do in the test. It was felt that Wales could win if they held their own at forward, but for better backs to succeed they had to have good ball and dry weather. However, there was doubt about the lasting ability of the All Blacks as they faded in this match but, what was most puzzling, was it by accident or design? Were they pulling our legs?

The All Blacks took the lead when Morris hit the upright with a penalty attempt after six minutes and the ball rebounded. Ebbw Vale failed to clear and Andy Haden was up to gather and crash over for a try that Morris easily converted. This score disturbed Gwent and set them back on the defensive but they gave little away and it was only 6–0 at the interval.

Morris, playing in only his second match of the tour, kicked a penalty and then dropped a lovely high forty yard goal to make it 12–0 before Pugh with his fourth attempt, landed a penalty for Gwent from 30 yards. A tapped penalty taken quickly saw the tourists move left and Stevens score in the corner but the crowd in that corner were not happy with the grounding of the ball and demonstrated that it was not a try. Morris failed to convert but at 16–3 the All Blacks were safe, only for Gwent to revive and hammer away.

Then we saw that the tourists were uncomfortable in defence and it was only just that Turner should get a try for the match to end at 16–7. Another victory, not really an impressive one, but such is the manner of any tour. After the match the team attended the official reception but left as soon as the speeches ended and returned to Porthcawl, ignoring the dance. This was an error. They should have requested two coaches, and Gwent even offered to provide an extra one and left half a dozen non-test players behind for the dance as a show of goodwill. Gwent officials were not pleased, neither were the hospitable folk of Ebbw Vale, and one could not blame them. Rugby tours are never all work and no play.

The All Blacks management then staged a selection meeting at Porthcawl and a special team meeting at midnight to announce the test XV and reserves. Strange people these New Zealanders ... midnight is the hour for dancing, wine tasting and romance ... even in test week. But Wales just had to be beaten and once the team was announced it is reported that 'all slept well!'

New Zealand nominated the strongest available fifteen and employed all the senior forwards including the three 'shop stewards', who were to precipitate the most dramatic action in New Zealand rugby. Wales had nominated in the previous week and the side was much as anticipated with only one new cap in Glyn Shaw, the 21-year-old loose head prop from Neath. The New Zealanders had nominated Johnny Johnson of the Metropolitan Police as the referee following a favourable match against Ulster. No Welshmen expected Mike Titcombe to be asked, but he would have been welcomed by the Welsh because he was never 'talked' into anything and had strong opinions on rough play. Although Johnson had control of a part of the 1970 England v. Wales match at Twickenham, he was almost unknown to most Welshmen, though well known to the London Welsh members of the side. He was, in fact, to play a vital part in the test. A vital decision was to be made by him, in all good faith, but in the opinion of many it was made in error!

The Welsh team had several doubtful starters through injury, with the most important of these being the chosen captain, British Lion Arthur Lewis of Ebbw Vale. In anticipation of his withdrawal, during the final practice on Thursday, I had advocated, strongly, the recall of former captain, John Dawes, and I still feel it would have been a wise decision. Not because Jim Shanklin who deputised for Lewis did not play well; in fact he worked hard, but because Dawes, with his vast experience, could well have controlled events more astutely behind the scrum and guided Wales to victory. Delme Thomas, in his first test as captain, was to do admirably, but it was just the fact that in the centre, Dawes' greater experience of leadership could well have turned the scales. As it was, Wales was to lose this tremendous struggle but prove the better rugby side. It was a hollow victory for New Zealand and a moral one for Wales, but the history books will always carry the score line in favour of N.Z. and one must regarded it as the poorest N.Z. side ever to beat Wales and take a four-three lead in the Principality.

Grant Batty for New Zealand and John Bevan for Wales had reported as doubtful starters on Wednesday but were passed fit on Thursday. As the experts on both sides and in both press camps, spilled out their words of forecast, the tension grew. Yet a decisive factor was the weather and as the rain continued to fall in Cardiff it made conditions more favourable for the All Blacks. Most critics read it this way, and added a rider that Karam might have an edge in place kicking.

New Zealand had the heavier, stronger forwards, and Wales had the better, faster backs. On a dry day it would be Wales; on a wet one, New Zealand. It was as cut and dried as that, even though the loyalists was adamant that 'their side' would win! On Friday hundreds of New Zealanders poured into the City with many still in search of tickets. Crawshays' Team held their annual V.P. dinner and there was much talk there of the match, as the rain fell. When I reached home and talked to my sons, Wayne and Gareth, I admitted to worrying more than usually about the weather because I felt Wales had the legs of New Zealand on a firm surface.

One was also worried about a possible lack of leadership behind, even though the new vice-captain, John Williams, was the most courageous man in the side. One was aware of his lack of experience in the job. More important still was the fact that Wales had become notoriously bad starters and tended to infringe technically before building up a full head of steam. I was more than usually moved towards pessimism, and when Saturday morning arrived still damp, I cursed the fact that Wales had the first test match of the tour, and argued that in future it must be in rotation. Yet Welshmen had waited since 1969 for this chance to obtain revenge, and none more so than coach Clive Rowlands, who had not shared directly in the Lions' triumph to 1971, and wanted so desperately to see Wales win.

Thirteenth Match
Versus Wales at Cardiff Arms Park National Stadium, December 2.
New Zealand won by five penalty goals and one try (19) to four penalty goals and one try (16).
Weather: Damp and showery. *Ground:* Good. *Crowd:* 50,000.
TEAMS:
WALES: J. P. R. Williams (*London Welsh*); T. G. R. Davies (*London Welsh*), J. L. Shanklin (*London Welsh*), R. T. Bergiers (*Llanelli*), J. C. Bevan (*Cardiff*); P. Bennett (*Llanelli*), G. O. Edwards (*Cardiff*); G. Shaw (*Neath*), J. Young (*London Welsh*), D. B. Llewelyn (*Llanelli*), W. D. Thomas (*Llanelli,* capt.), D. L. Quinnell (*Llanelli*), W. D. Morris (*Neath*), T. M. Davies (*Swansea*), J. Taylor (*London Welsh*).
NEW ZEALAND: J. F. Karam; B. G. Williams, D. A. Hales, R. M. Parkinson, G. B. Batty; R. E. Burgess, S. M. Going; J. D. Matheson, R. W. Norton, K. Murdoch, H. H. McDonald, P. J. Whiting, A. J. Wyllie, A. R. Sutherland, I. A. Kirkpatrick (capt.). *Replacement:* A. I. Scown for Wyllie.
Referee: R. F. Johnson (England).

Tickets emerged for sale a few hours before the kick off, following a famine during the week but the weather accounted for this as many followers, in the final reckoning, preferred the warmth of their lounges and colour TV to the crowded, wet terraces of the world's most historic rugby ground. In this changing world, where comfort and the easy life tend to dominate, this is not surprising, but there must have been long queues down Westgate Street in 1905 and many locked outside. If all those who have said, since the day, that they saw that historic match, then there were 100,000 present, twice as many as in 1972! The latest crowd sang well despite the rain, and cheered loudly as the teams fielded. The great moment had arrived and everything each country could have done to prepare their teams for the struggle had been done. Now it was up to the players and the referee, and everyone at the ground REALLY wanted an exciting, clean match, full of good rugby and no nonsense.

From the moment Bennett kicked off for Wales towards the Westgate Street end, Wales played in second gear, as if nonplussed or, to use a modern phrase, under the influence. One wit near the Press Box suggested it was a 'fix'! Known as notoriously bad starters, Wales were six points down in nine minutes through two safely placed penalty goals by Joe Karam, who was to become the New Zealand hero of the day.

First, in the second minute, Morris got up too quickly from the second scrum of the match, on the Welsh '25', and Karam kicked an easy goal. After eight minutes there was a scrum offence by hooker Young and Karam kicked a 30-yard goal to give the All Blacks the early lead they needed. Bennett kicked wide with a 47-yard attempt for Wales, and Bevan made two good saves near the left touch-line from high kicks ahead, while Burgess was kicking well to keep Williams running from touch-line to touch-line at full-back.

New Zealand went further ahead after 18 minutes with a try and Welsh spirits were indeed low. This was a telling blow since Wales had looked little like an international side and the play had indeed been one-sided!

Receiving from a line-out on the Welsh '25', Going punted high over his pack in line with the right touch-line. Bevan collected the ball but couldn't hold it as he was rushed by Going, and the ball went loose towards the Welsh goal line. Williams went to steer it into touch but the All Blacks forwards drove through, Murdoch gathered, was knocked down by Bennett, of all people, and then rolled over the Welsh goal line. Was it a try? Referee Johnson was up with the play and signalled a try but Karam could not convert it, and Wales were ten points in arrears in 18 minutes – not a healthy situation and the crowd was dazed by such a state of affairs.

Four minutes later the opening blows were tempered a little by Bennett succeeding with his second attempt at a penalty goal from 25 yards, and it was 10–3, only for Wales to concede another penalty at a set scrum in the easiest of positions on their own '25' and the sure-footed Karam kicked his third goal. At 13–3, Wales were still ten points behind.

There was something wrong with the Welsh side; they were not really together and were not tidying up at the line-out, while Johnson was generally at the back of the line and not viewing the infringements in front. A pass from Edwards to the blind side went astray and the All Blacks were almost in again. They were on top at this stage and, when the interval arrived, Bennett was still clearing under pressure, and we were left wondering in the Press Box as to why Wales were making it so easy for a straighforward New Zealand team. They deserved to lead, but not by ten points. The main trouble for Wales had been their failure to get enough ball, good or bad, and the conceding of penalties in kickable positions. Referee Johnson appeared to some of us strangely reluctant, as he had been in Belfast, to scrutinise more accurately Going's put into the scrum.

Poor Clive Rowlands was suffering in the Committee Box and, as he told me afterwards, 'We had stick from the referees in New Zealand and now on our ground we received the same treatment,' and then with a smile added, 'Can you recall any N.Z. referee giving New Zealand's opponents in test matches penalties on the N.Z. "25"!' At that moment he must have felt the world was against him but he was man enough to say, later, 'Wales played so much below form in the first half.'

Edwards was hurt soon after the restart but recovered and after five minutes Wales got the try they wanted. N.Z. won a tight head but Edwards robbed Going as he attempted to collect the ball to the open side. Edwards booted through and it rebounded to Bennett who cleverly gathered and sent Shanklin away to give Bevan a 40-yard run for the left corner with two men, Williams and Karam to beat. In a thrilling run, Bevan got to the corner for a fine try but Bennett could not convert it.

Four minutes later, Bennett kicked a 35-yard goal for a line-out offence and it was 13–10. One felt the whole crowd lift and the match assumed a totally different atmosphere and, from one of Welsh concession, it moved to one of stern challenge. It was the All Blacks' turn to be under pressure and the Welsh forwards suddenly knitted into a complete unit, casting off the bedraggled grey coat of lethargy and donning the dominant one of shining scarlet.

Then came a tragic decision. Delme Thomas fielded a kick; the New Zealand forwards, inside the ten yards area, continued running on to him and were thus offside, but Llewelyn then joined Thomas and was adjudged ahead of him and it was he who was penalised. This was a decisive error. Karam kicked a perfect goal from 42 yards and it was 16–10, forcing Wales to score at least twice to win. Hopes were raised for the

Welsh, two minutes later, when Bevan was obstructed and Bennett kicked a 30-yard goal to make it 16–13.

Karam had another shot when Wales fell offside at a maul but this time, kicked wide. Perhaps the tide was turning but another penalty at a scrum, this time for not binding, as Referee Johnson was to explain later, gave Karam another chance from 44 yards. The 'wonder boy' of the day made no mistake and it was 19–13 with 16 minutes plus injury time remaining. Wales, like a wounded dragon, raised its head for the final onslaught. New Zealand were tiring in front and two penalties to them and two to Wales brought forth no place kicks, but New Zealand were resorting to tactics 'outside' the spirit and the laws to prevent Wales getting the try they were seeking. Gerald Davies and John Bevan were brought down after kicking but Johnson issued no warnings.

Then came the real turning point in the match when Wales had a good try disallowed and this error was to prove more than decisive at the end of the match. The fact that it was disallowed by Referee Johnson led to a controversy that erased from the record books N.Z.'s claim about the Dean's 'try' of 1905. It was rather sad for Johnson and Wales, and indeed New Zealand, since it *was* a try and at the end of the match few really believed New Zealand were the better side. Yet the victory in points was forgotten in the sensational events that followed in the early hours of the next morning.

Wales were attacking in the 29th minute of the second half when Delme Thomas fielded the ball just inside the New Zealand '25' and made a good deal of ground till he was held. Thomas slipped the ball to Williams, who was knocked down and NOT tackled just short of the line. Williams was not *tackled or held by one or more opponents so that while he was tackled the ball touched the ground*. He crawled forward over the line and scored in accordance with Law 18, Section 4.

Referee Johnson should have allowed the try which would have been deserved and proved the turning point in the game. Immediately afterwards, it was played and replayed on TV and many times in the days that followed. Experts argued, but having watched the tele-recordings and listened to the views of experts, including many former and present international referees from several countries, some of whom had a better view than myself, since it was in the far right corner, opposite to the press box, I am convinced it was a try.

Let me put it simply, and not as a question of 'sour grapes', because even though the New Zealanders won in points, there was for them no glory in the victory: either Murdoch's allowed try and Williams' disallowed try were BOTH valid or invalid. The inconsistency of Mr Johnson played too important a part, however unintentional, in the outcome of the match. At least the 'Deans incident' and inquest was at last closed!

Wales took a tapped penalty instead of a kick at goal before, after 38 minutes, Bennett landed a 30-yard goal, when Davies was again obstructed. New Zealand had really 'had it' at this stage. The Welsh pack were on top and pushed them back at the set scrums. The crowd yelled encouragement and 'willed' a try to win the match, but it was not to be.

Finally, John Williams, joining the line and kicking ahead was obstructed, and Bennett had a last chance in injury time to square the match. From 30 yards out and a widish angle, the ball appeared to be going over and then drifted outside the post. A gallant attempt had failed and the final whistle went. A weary and indeed fortunate N.Z. side, lacking in the higher sense of sportsmanship, (which had highlighted the 1935 side when they were losing in the final minutes of that match) left the field. There was no cheering, only a sense of disappointment, not so much at suffering defeat, but that the Welsh XV had proved the better rugby side and that New Zealand seemed ready to do anything rather than lose. They lost many friends in the final twenty minutes of this tremendous struggle, but little did we realise what was to follow. N.Z. press members just told me, 'We were lucky to get away with that!' So they were!

7 *Dial M for Murdoch*

Welshmen walked from the Cardiff Arms Park quite bewildered because they could not accept the fact that they had lost to what they considered to be an inferior side. They felt that the penalty goal difference was not realistic and that Wales in the second half had done enough to deserve the victory. They were not happy at the result and, while they conceded that Wales committed several technical infringements and lost, New Zealand, especially in the last twenty minutes, committed physical infringements and won. It was not a victory based on quality or real rugby values.

Again, many felt that Sid Going enjoyed a charmed life in putting the ball into the scrum and that Mr Johnson appeared somewhat inconsistent in his application of the law. I felt this was in no way intentional but that he may have been 'carried away' by the pressure of the moment. An extremely pleasant fellow and a good rugger man, he was said to be rather tense before the start, which is quite understandable, for it was regarded as something like a match for the championship of the World. Personally I could not agree with this view after the series of defeats suffered by New Zealand in the previous twenty-four months.

Reflecting upon this match, New Zealand looked a mere shadow of the great All Blacks teams of previous tours, and Wales missed a great chance of victory as they were the better rugby side. In recent years Wales have been a second half team but have come good in the last ten minutes before the interval. In this match they were certainly late in gathering momentum and by half time were 13–3 down. Yet they made it 19–16 before the close and most Welshmen would have settled for 19–19, as indeed would several New Zealand supporters I spoke to afterwards, for they believed this would have been a just result.

In the *Western Mail* I discussed the need for the direct and indirect penalty in rugby football, with a kick at goal for foul play and a free kick, but not at goal, for the smaller technical infringements. Vivian Jenkins and myself have been campaigning for this since 1959 when New Zealand won by six penalty goals to four tries against the British Lions. Obviously, this match at Cardiff more than suggested that there must be stiffer penalties for blatant obstruction in one's own half, than for the mere raising of a foot a split second early in the set scrum. The offences bear no comparison in their effect upon the spirit of the game.

The New Zealand press left the box in no gay-hearted mood, for they must have realised that the All Blacks had merely survived, and had brought no further glory to their country. Few will forget those last twenty minutes and it was an unhappy day. Worse, however, was to follow.

The dinner in honour of the teams followed the match and was a most enjoyable affair. Officials from both countries spoke pleasantly and Ian Kirkpatrick pronounced Mr Johnson's effort as the best refereeing he had ever experienced. There were seven N.Z. press members invited to the dinner but only two appeared, senior men Terry McLean and Bob Irvine, and two Welshmen, Ron Griffiths and myself. It was an excellent meal enjoyed by all and, especially a healthy-looking top table of members from the four home unions and French officials together with V.I.P.'s. Both teams sang and all was friendly. The Welsh players accepted their defeat and extreme disappointment exceedingly well, although I saw Clive Rowlands, perhaps the most disappointed of all, wince a little during the speeches, for he really wanted his side to win to avenge 1969.

After the dinner, the guests and players retired to various parts of the hotel and it is reported that seven or eight New Zealanders attended the dance and enjoyed. it. However, the first jarring note occurred when a member of the N.Z. party was most rude to the assistant manager Bob Duff in the reception room. Thankfully, Bob Duff, as a gentleman, walked away to prevent a 'scene', but I understand the player concerned was censured the next day.

The midnight hour was passed, into the 'day of rest', but

then came the start of the major 'incident' of the tour. The burly 17 st. prop, Keith Murdoch, of Otago, previously named the 'wild man' of N.Z. rugby, celebrated, as indeed would any player after winning a Test, if he enjoyed his beer! However, Murdoch, it seemed, was getting out of hand and becoming, to use a polite word, difficult. This is, of course, not a fault that is confined just to New Zealanders, and no one seeks to suggest that all other countries have 'angels' on and off the field. Murdoch, however, was starting to prove an embarrassment to his management and many of his fellows.

At this stage it is necessary to explain that the three strong men of the side, Sutherland, Wyllie and Murdoch, aided by the 'silent one', Sid Going, and, to a lesser degree, the young Grant Batty, appeared to want to influence the running of the tour. One suspected that they were trying to influence Kirkpatrick who, to me, appeared a most pleasant fellow. They were called the 'Mafia' by the British press and instead of encouraging the younger players in the art of public relations, they gave the impression of being less communicative than previous wearers of the All Blacks' blazer.

The management may have made errors, as did the players, but several people important in the rugby world, described to me in detail how they tried to make polite conversation with one member of the side. Often, he did not even answer, and sometimes turned his back and moved away. Was this the way a tourist should behave? He may have been a good player, but he was no ambassador for New Zealand and, even if one excused him on the grounds of shyness, he cannot be forgiven his bad manners and lack of courtesy on this tour.

Murdoch had steadily been building up a real reputation for himself and his conversation at dinner after the London Counties match with Sir William Ramsay was a 'classic'. Murdoch was given to grunted replies when he did answer, no matter be it to children, supporters, press or officials; this was a most 'endearing' habit!

The jungle drums were beating through the British Isles and the 'rumours' returned to base as the rather strange bunch of travellers calling themselves the Seventh All Blacks moved from hotel to hotel, and played match after match. Wallace Reyburn called the Sixth All Blacks the 'Unsmiling Giants', a splendid phrase, but the Seventh All Blacks made the Sixth look like a team of laughing policemen. At an early stage, I felt sorry for the management and captain, who always treated me with the greatest courtesy, and young men like Bob Burgess, Bruce Robertson, Alaister Scown, Trevor Morris, Lyn Colling and others. It was to be a team of two sections . . . the friendly ones and others!

It was at the University Arms, Cambridge that I experienced the first 'incident' when a group of non-playing 'revellers' tore down some lift signs early on the morning of the match. It was approximately 4 a.m. and the noise awoke Gwen and myself. The next morning I noticed some clean new wallpaper where the notice had been and, later in the day, was told of the occurence by a member of the hotel staff. Still, I did not pay too much attention to this, as many a Lion has broken a window or a door, or even smashed a glass or two! But I kept it in mind in case there followed a series of 'incidents'. On tour one tends to disregard rumours but what happened at Cardiff early on Sunday morning, December 3, 1972 shocked the rugby world.

Murdoch was, it seems, on the 'prowl' but in more determined mood than ever the 'wreckers and burners' of the 1968 Lions tour, or the All Blacks in the North British Hotel after Colin Meads had been sent off in 1967. He charged through groups and eventually 'invaded' the kitchen, this resulting in trays of glasses going all over the place, and causing guests to make a hasty retreat! The kitchen staff, mostly female, was terrified, as a result of which members of a local security guard firm, employed by the hotel management to deal with possible disturbances, were called to the kitchen.

The security guard involved, Peter Grant, tells the story as follows: 'I was called to the kitchen because Murdoch was harassing waitresses and other members of the staff by demanding food and drink, and behaving in an unruly manner. With another guard, I asked Murdoch to leave but as he was not prepared to leave peacefully, we sent for Mr Ernie Todd. When he arrived and put his hand on Murdoch's shoulder, the player appeared to prepare to strike him. We then restrained Murdoch and some of his team mates arrived and said they could handle him. We withdrew but as they came out of the kitchen, I was talking to one of the other players and thought Murdoch had gone but, suddenly, bang, he struck me from behind a pillar. I was dazed but eventually Murdoch was taken away.'

One can easily imagine the confusion caused by this incident, but fortunately, in the hotel at the time were John Tallent, chairman of the Four Home Unions Tours Committee, and its secretary, Albert Agar, both excellent and experienced officials. On Sunday morning the big 'inquest' began before the team set off for Birmingham, and the vital interview was between Manager Todd and the player, Keith Murdoch.

Poor Ernie Todd was faced with a problem, for Murdoch had suddenly become a 'risk', and so he had to decide, and his decision was to 'send Murdoch home for his own good and for the sake of the team.' He was in touch with the NZRU but unfortunately the team for the next match had already been released and contained the name of Murdoch as prop. NZPA representative, John Brooks, had passed it on to London and it reached P.A. for circulation to all papers in accordance with his tour brief.

It was not altered by the time Ernie Todd issued his statement on Monday morning that Murdoch was returning, but there was *never* any intention on Todd's part to deceive the British public or, of suddenly changing his mind about Murdoch, and this should be stated in his defence. He had a most difficult task to perform and he made the right decision, for Murdoch was clearly a P.R. 'risk'. In a few days, the NZRU Council fully endorsed Ernie Todd's decision.

Monday's evening papers all over the country were full of the Murdoch story, although the *Western Mail* had scooped the mornings by carrying an interview with, and picture of, Peter Grant, the security guard. The 'activity' was transferred from the sports desks of the national papers to the news desks. News reporters and cameramen went into action and 'trailed' Murdoch from the Birmingham hotel to London Airport, seeking pictures and interviews, while radio and TV descended upon Peter Grant in Monmouthshire.

When Tuesday morning's papers rolled off the presses, Murdoch's case was in the headlines, and he received more publicity than any rugby player in history, because he had made 'history'. The headlines in a bewildered New Zealand were the same size type as those announcing the declaration of war!

Murdoch flew out of Heathrow Airport at 5.30 p.m. on Monday, almost into oblivion, as that was the last heard or seen of him until long after the tourists left Britain.

He left the plane at Singapore and defied all efforts to trace him. It takes a lot for an 17 st. prop to disappear into thin air, but Mr Murdoch did. Why, I wonder? The British Press laid into his 'misdeeds' and the New Zealand Press at home were divided upon this case. Always extremely sensitive about their rugby, some New Zealanders proclaimed Murdoch was a great guy on and off the field, but there were enough to suggest otherwise!

The most serious condemnation of both Murdoch's approach and N.Z. rugby came from Dudley Manning, the much respected Sports Editor and rugby correspondent of the *Otago Daily News*, the most influential paper in Murdoch's own province. Mr Manning wrote:

'Murdoch is where he is at the moment because the N.Z.R.U. establishment put him there. Something stinks in New Zealand rugby when a player is wanted in an All Black side solely for the purpose of straightening-up an opponent. A selector wanted Murdoch to play against the Lions in 1971 'to straighten things up in the front row with a bit of Knuckle.'

Murdoch was selected to play for Otago and in three tests against the Lions, but withdrew from all of them, allegedly injured, and became the 'mystery' player of the year. When he was selected for the last test team, announced in a crowded Eden Park, Auckland, club house there were cries of dissent from many N.Z.R.U. members, as I recall the occasion vividly.

In Birmingham, Ernie Todd, obviously tired and fed up with the whole business and, perhaps, disappointed at the play of his side and the lack of praise meted out to his team in beating Wales, which was his 'one ambition' before he left New Zealand, made a P.R. error. He accused the British Press (and that means all of the 'papers) of conducting a smear campaign against his team. This was indeed unwise and rather unfair even if some 'papers *had* given the Murdoch case the treatment!

It was a remark untypical of Mr Todd, who one regarded as a wise businessman, and he should have thought quickly of his own 'papers at home and recounted some of their exploits. He should have thought of what the travelling N.Z. Press had said about Welsh rugby in New Zealand and South Africa, after the Cardiff match, (and I have the cuttings to prove it!).

Still, two wrongs do not make a right, and as Murdoch 'vanished' the tour continued with a defeat at Moseley, but a much better 'after the match' reaction. Sid Going was seen in conversation with Arthur Rees, the Chief Constable of Staffordshire, chairman of Crawshays Rugby Club, and a former Welsh pack leader, who helped Wales to victory over New Zealand in 1935. Things were looking up. Perhaps the 1972 All Blacks would make it. Perhaps Murdoch had not vanished in vain!

An example of the difficult service Scottish scrum half Ian McCrae received from the line-outs, as a result of untidy tapping back by his forwards

Alex Wyllie storms his way through to score New Zealands' first try against Scotland at Murrayfield

England v New Zealand at Twickenham – and the legs are having to stretch. Note two white shirts to six All Blacks, which is the clue to the New Zealand victory

8 *The Aftermath—and Murrayfield*

All sorts of rumours emerged from the tourists' hotel at Birmingham, but they visited Rugby School and practised on its famous playing fields. They viewed the plaque commemorating the brave deed of young William Webb Ellis who, like so many worthy Englishmen, is buried in France. The game as we know it today, owes Ellis much in legend, if not in fact, and all of us, in all countries other than England, should pay homage to the man and his country for setting in motion or, if one prefers a time honoured cliché, of planting the acorn which is now a vast oak tree spreading its branches healthily throughout the world.

I commend my good friend Uel Titley's work on the *History of the RFU* for, as an old Rugbiean, he writes with genuine love and tenderness about the deeds and life of W.W.E. and the Game's development at Rugby School. For one who has lived with rugby all one's life, I salute those young men of Rugby School and those who followed at Cheltenham College, Guy's Hospital and Oxford and Cambridge Universities. These noble institutions were the true cradles of the game and New Zealanders and Welshmen would do well to remember this!

I trust the All Blacks appreciated this and lost a little of their tenseness at Rugby School trying to forget, as they were, the unhappy Murdoch incident. The practice session was not an outstanding one, for poor Trevor Morris, one of the nicest members of the party, could not regain his place-kicking form. Likeable Bob Duff, complete with woollen skull cap, retained his stoical calm, thinking, perhaps, that life was much more peaceful and, possibly, more enjoyable in his home city of Christchurch!

A man of few words, Bob Duff is not an extrovert. Perhaps, in this modern world of ballyhoo and 'bull', he was too nice a man, too serious, and too gentle to bully the recalcitrant members of his party. I wonder? Duff was my idea of a good New Zealander – no chip on the shoulder.

The West Midlands side looked good on paper and led by David Duckham it promised trouble for the All Blacks if it could play running rugby, but the Moseley ground had been given a thorough soaking by incessant rain. Fortunately, groundsman Flack and his staff from Edgbaston worked hard to make it playable and for ten minutes it was in good condition, at least good enough to enable the West Midlands to make a flying start!

Fourteenth Match
Versus West Midlands at Moseley, December 6.
West Midlands won by one goal, one dropped goal, one penalty goal and one try (16) to two tries (8).
Weather: Fine. *Ground:* Very soft. *Crowd:* 10,000.
TEAMS:
WEST MIDLANDS: S. A. Doble (*Moseley*); D. J. Duckham (*Coventry*, capt.), P. C. Preece (*Coventry*), M. K. Swain (*Moseley*), M. J. Cooper (*Moseley*); J. F. Finlan (*Moseley*), J. Webster (*Moseley*); T. F. Corless (*Birmingham*), J. D. Gray (*Coventry*), K. E. Fairbrother (*Coventry*), N. E. Horton (*Moseley*), L. Smith (*Moseley*), I. N. Pringle (*Moseley*), J. C. White (*Moseley*), T. M. Cowell (*Rugby*).
NEW ZEALAND: T. J. Morris; G. R. Skudder, I. A. Hurst, M. Sayers, B. G. Williams; R. E. Burgess, G. L. Colling; K. K. Lambert, R. A. Urlich, G. J. Whiting, A. M. Haden, I. A. Eliason, K. W. Stewart, B. E. Holmes, I. A. Kirkpatrick (capt.).
Referee: R. Lewis (Llangynwyd).

It was a remarkable start, probably the best of the whole tour against the tourists, even more decisive than at Llanelli, for the West Midlands attacked from the kick-off and moved the ball accurately and swiftly to give the tourists the real 'run around.' As a result, thirteen points were scored in the opening seven minutes.

First the ball came back to Finlan in the second minute, some 30 yards out, and he steadied to drop a lovely high goal. Then followed quick possession in the loose and the ball moved like a rocket to left wing Cooper, enjoying a slight overlap, and with a scurrying dash he was over in the corner for an excellent try. Next time the ball went out to the right and there was the flaxen-haired Duckham in full flight for the right corner. Another fine try and big Sam Doble kicked the goal. This was amazing; 13 points in seven minutes against the All Blacks!

Soon there appeared small brown patches on the green field that grew bigger and browner with every scrum and line-out, to suggest that soon it would become a hard forward slog if the All Blacks steadied and recovered. The West Midlands' backs had enjoyed their moment of glory and taken their chances brilliantly. Their first ten minutes of running rugby had decided the day, but what was to follow was hard and exciting!

Gradually the All Blacks got into an attacking position and a delayed clearing kick was charged down to give Mark Sayers a chance to dive on the ball for a try and make it 13–4, but big Sam Doble landed a penalty goal and it was 16–4 at the interval. Could the All Blacks get back 12 points playing down the hill in the mud? It could be done, but would need a special effort.

They tried hard enough, but it was a lack of sophistication in attack, determined Midlands defence close to the scrum and ruck, and a Midland pack and scrum half, Jan Webster, that refused to be beaten. It was good stuff in the mud, clean, and often exciting, as referee Ron Lewis, of Wales, kept a firm grip on things. He awarded 20 penalties to the All Blacks and nine to the Midlands, but almost all were for technical infringements. The All Blacks were too ruck-conscious to win and their wings, Williams and Skudder, were starved yet again. Colling played á la Going, and Burgess made only two real breaks despite much good possession. It was played back to the forwards too often, too tightly and the Midlands' defence was never stretched as it should have been.

The All Blacks remained predictable, collecting only one more try through Hurst despite regular possession, and so fell to the third defeat of the tour at 16–8. The West Midlands were delighted with themselves and especially David Duckham, who, like Delme Thomas, of Llanelli, was pleased to repeat the 1971 triumphs.

New Zealand were depressed at first with their defeat, but showed a marked improvement in their P.R. approach, for players and officials mixed freely in the Moseley clubhouse for half an hour before leaving for the official reception. This was more like it – in victory or defeat, show the flag, for everyone appreciates it.

So it was on to Bradford with the news that Lindsay Clark, also of Otago, and aged 30, would be flying over to join the party as substitute for Keith Murdoch. He was delighted with his selection, but sorry for the man he replaced who, at this stage, had vanished into thin air. Allegedly, he had got off at Singapore, without moustache, for a rest and, as the days went by, nothing more was heard of him, although later his mother was to report to Ian Wooldridge of the *Daily Mail* in a telephone conversation that she had heard from her son.

The North Eastern Countries included a couple of internationals, and one player, Ian McGeechan, who was to be capped for Scotland a week later. They had spirit and felt they would give the tourists a hard game, even though the All Blacks had in action eleven members of the side which played in the Welsh Test.

Fifteenth Match
Versus North East Counties at Bradford, December 9.
New Zealand won by one goal and one dropped goal (9) to one penalty goal (3).
Weather: Cold and wet. *Ground:* Slippery. *Crowd:* 12,000.
TEAMS:
NORTH EAST COUNTIES: B. Patrick (*Gosforth*); D. Carr (*Gosforth*), I. McGeechan (*Headingley*, capt.), P. Warfield (*Durham University*), A. Cheshire (*Hartlepool*); A. Old (*Leicester*), M. Young (*Gosforth*); C. White (*Northern*), D. Madsen (*Gosforth*), P. McLoughlin (*Gosforth*), J. Hall (*Cheltenham*), R. Uttley (*Gosforth*), R. Leathley (*Halifax*), T. Donovan (*Headingley*), P. Nash (*Middlesbrough*).
NEW ZEALAND: J. F. Karam; B. G. Williams, I. A. Hurst, R. M. Parkinson, G. B. Batty; I. N. Stevens, S. M. Going; J. D. Matheson, R. W. Norton, G. J. Whiting, P. J. Whiting, A. M. Haden, I. A. Kirkpatrick (capt.), A. R. Sutherland, A. I. Scown. *Replacement:* G. R. Skudder for Batty.
Referee: F. Palade (France).

The North East gave the heavier All Blacks a hard game and N.Z. reporter with the team, Bob Howitt, suggested, 'The All Blacks' scrum was 11,000 miles short of Test match precision. That is about the distance Keith Murdoch is from the

All Blacks' team. Without the 17 st. prop their scrum wasn't a scrum against the North East. Against a pack conceding almost two stone a man the All Blacks were rudely buckled in the opening minutes. This led to Matheson switching to tight head with Graham Whiting, after which the scrummaging improved without ever becoming good. It was alarming to see the New Zealanders tossed about in the scrums.'

Kirkpatrick told Howitt that he thought the Counties front row should have been penalised for illegal tactics which upset his team, but the referee, a Frenchman, could not understand what he was talking about, 'while I did not understand anything he explained!'

It was an extremely close for the All Blacks as the Counties produced the best tackling of the tour up to this stage and one of the tacklers-in-chief, the 21-year-old Durham University student Peter Warfield, won his first England cap (in the match against the All Blacks) as a result of this heartening performance.

Matheson experienced a hard time of it against Fieldlam McLoughlin, brother of Lion Ray, who had been well 'advised' by his powerful and knowledgeable brother. So it was in the scrums and through hard tackling that the Counties made a match of it and had the All Blacks battling to avoid their fourth defeat.

Again, the tourists appeared more than unusually disturbed by the dull, bitingly cold weather of Lidgett Green. They dropped many a pass and were hustled off the ball. The tackling and covering was superb and could not have been bettered, but both sides missed chances.

Had Old been able to keep his feet he would have kicked a penalty goal from in front of the posts, and perhaps have dropped a goal. Some critics present doubted whether the throw-in from touch was straight that led to Batty scoring a try. It was not a great day for the All Blacks and suggested they were going to have few of them on the tour. They were winning many more matches than they were losing, but not winning convincingly. Little Joe Karam was still doing a noble job at full back and Sid Going was always a menace at scrum-half. Yet this ordinary display in difficult conditions served to inspire the people north of the border in Scotland, although injuries to the Scottish 'chosen' kept pace with those of the

All Blacks. Scorers at Bradford were Old with a penalty goal for the North East, and Batty a try converted by Karam and Going a dropped goal.

The next stop was Glasgow, over the hills but not so far away, where they met a combined Glasgow and Edinburgh side – minus those players selected to appear in the Saturday test – at Hughenden, Glasgow, on the Tuesday – the same day as a disappointing Varsity Match was played at Twickenham. Ian Kirkpatrick decided to take a rest, having appeared in 11 of the first 13 matches and Wyllie, captain of Canterbury, took over with Sutherland at No. 8. Robertson came back into the side for the first time following his injury at Cardiff and it was hoped he would prove himself fit enough to play in the Test against Scotland. His thumb was right, but a hamstring pull had been suffered by the unlucky player in the previous week. Lindsay Clark, the replacement for Murdoch, joined the team and Manager Todd heaved a sigh of relief on seeing the blond prop, but his propping troubles were far from over! The combined side included several players of promise and the best of these were Hay at full back, Forsyth at centre, Dall at outside-half and Wright at lock, while an Englishman, Mr Welsby of Lancashire, had charge of the match.

Sixteenth Match
Versus Glasgow and Edinburgh at Hughenden, December 12.
Weather: Fine. *Ground:* Firm and well grassed. *Crowd:* 5,000.
TEAMS:
GLASGOW and EDINBURGH: B. Hay (*Boroughmuir FP*); R. S. M. Hannah (*West of Scotland*), M. D. Hunter (*Glasgow HSFP*), I. Forsyth (*Stewart's FP*), S. L. Briggs (*Edinburgh Wanderers*); F. N. F. Dall (*Heriot's FP*), D. W. Morgan (*Melville FP*, capt.); J. Craig (*Ayr*), Q. Dunlop (*West of Scotland*), D. S. D. McCallum (*Jordanhill*), R. W. Wright (*Edinburgh Wanderers*), R. S. Tolbert (*Watsonians*), T. Young (*West of Scotland*), G. M. Strachan (*Jordanhill*), W. S. Watson (*Boroughmuir FP*).
NEW ZEALAND: J. F. Karam; G. R. Skudder, B. J. Robertson, M. Sayers, D. A. Hales; R. E. Burgess, G. L. Colling; K. K. Lambert, R. A. Urlich, J. D. Matheson, A. M. Haden, H. H. Macdonald, A. J. Wyllie (capt.), A. R. Sutherland, K. W. Stewart. *Replacement:* P. J. Whiting for Haden.
Referee: A. Welsby (Lancashire).

The All Blacks won again, but only just, and they had another dose of their own tactical 'medicine', as Manager Ernie Todd readily admitted. Ian Kirkpatrick, watching anxiously from the stand, commented, 'Well, it was a win!' And all the party, those on and off the field, must have been relieved that another midweek defeat was not suffered, as seemed possible at one stage.

Todd agreed that the Cities' tactics of lying up in defence, waiting for opposing errors and not risking too many moves of their own, were often employed at home in New Zealand, both in the inter-provincial matches and against touring teams. I can vouch for this and believe it was this factor – New Zealand's confrontation with their own tactics for the first time in the British Isles – that was one of the major reasons for their own failure to sparkle on the field of play.

The combined side really made the All Blacks work for their win, which came only towards the end and this, after they had enjoyed a major share of the possession! However, they retained their unbeaten record in Scotland and this was something. A defeat in this match would have lowered morale before the Test, yet the decisive try was a little doubtful, and City players were convinced that a brave full-back, Bruce Hay, the hero of the match, had touched down before Alan Sutherland, the best of the All Blacks on the day. They did not regard it as a try but, when the whistle for time was blown, the All Blacks were home by a goal, two penalties and a try to two penalty goals and a try. When injury time was entered, the score was 12–10 and, as David Irvine pointed out in *The Guardian*, 'the message was clear at the end, no game on this tour will be easy from now on, particularly while the All Blacks persist in creating difficulties for themselves.'

The combined side took the lead in the first-half when Robertson, returning to the side, did not enjoy the cold and a dropped pass by him was kicked upfield by Forsyth. Then Skudder failed to cover the rolling ball and threequarters Hannah and Hunter were up together quickly to send the most promising back in Scotland, Fraser Dall, over in the corner for a try. It was not converted and, although little Joe Karam kicked a penalty for New Zealand before the interval, the Cities changed over one point ahead which surprised even their most rabid of supporters. This was an indication of the growing strength of Scottish rugby through its greater depth and the application to coaching.

Early in the second-half, Haden breached the Cities defence from a tapped penalty and although he was stopped, Urlich was up to gather and score for Karam to convert. Then Haden limped off and was replaced by Peter Whiting. As Haden did not appear to be seriously hurt, a few suggested this was a 'tactical substitution.' Whiting neutralised young Wright, who had been jumping so well for the Cities and had given Haden no joy at all. It may have been quite legal, of course, but the Scots are always fussy about such happenings. You've got to be really injured in Scotland to be replaced, as we were to find out in the Test a few days later!

Morgan then reduced the arrears with a penalty goal from 50 yards for the Cities, followed by one from Karam and another from Morgan to leave it 10–12 at the start of injury time. It was still touch and go before the throw-in and the try by Sutherland that made it 10–16. Victory to the All Blacks, but a lot of glory to the Cities with a considerably below-strength team. In the record book it was a win, and the start of the second-half of the tour. The All Blacks did not want to lose any more matches.

They moved on to Edinburgh for the second test of the tour and Bruce Robertson was in their XV to meet Scotland together with Burgess and Sutherland. The outside-half injured a leg in Glasgow and was forced to withdraw and Sutherland developed influenza which was to keep him out of the test and the next two matches.

Scotland had similar worries with injured players and the big centre John Frame withdrew while Gordon Brown at lock was a doubtful starter. The All Blacks management played it cool and although they must have known that Burgess and Sutherland would not make it, they did not announce the changes until Saturday morning.

Terry McLean, in a cable home, suggested that the team's arrival in the beautiful city of Edinburgh could be the turning point of the tour. The corner needed turning as a few days previously McLean had quoted one of the young All Blacks as saying, 'We haven't come here to make friends!' This was a truism; they rarely, if ever, appeared to do so. However, with the second test came the chance for the team to prove better than it appeared, both in ability and manners.

Seventeenth Match
Versus Scotland at Murrayfield, December 16.
New Zealand won by one goal and two tries (14) to two penalties and one dropped goal (9).
Weather: Fine. *Ground:* Firm. *Crowd:* 60,000.
TEAMS:
SCOTLAND: A. R. Irvine (*Heriot's FP*); W. C. C. Steele (*Bedford*), I. W. Forsyth (*Stewart's College FP*), J. M. Renwick (*Hawick*), D. Shedden (*West of Scotland*); I. R. McGeechan (*Headingley*), I. G. MacCrae (*Gordonians*); I. McLauchlan (*Jordanhill*), R. L. Clark (*Edinburgh Wanderers*), A. B. Carmichael (*West of Scotland*), A. F. McHarg (*West of Scotland*), G. L. Brown (*West of Scotland*), N. A. MacEwan (*Gala*), P. C. Brown (*Gala*, capt.), R. J. Arneil (*Northampton*).
NEW ZEALAND: J. F. Karam; B. G. Williams, B. J. Robertson, R. M. Parkinson, G. B. Batty; R. E. Burgess, S. M. Going; J. D. Matheson, R. W. Norton, G. J. Whiting, P. J. Whiting, H. H. Macdonald, I. A. Kirkpatrick (capt.), A. R. Sutherland, A. J. Wyllie. *Replacement*: K. K. Lambert for Matheson.
Referee: G. Domercq (France).

Sixty thousand spectators were present when the teams fielded. The first incident was a 58-yard attempt at penalty goal by Joe Karam which fell short, and soon after Jeff Matheson was injured in a maul. He was assisted from the field and taken to hospital with a badly damaged rib cage that was to prevent him playing again on the tour. Matheson was in such pain as he was helped to the touch line that there was no discussion regarding a replacement and Kent Lambert took the field to win his first cap at the age of 20. However, the only two fit All Blacks' props were on the field, while Bruce Robertson, in the centre, with both thighs heavily strapped, did not appear to be too fit. Burgess, of course, had cried off with a leg injury and Alan Sutherland with the flu. Thus, the All Blacks were not really at full strength, being without Murdoch, Matheson, Sutherland and Burgess from the side that narrowly defeated Wales. The game was therefore a test for the reserves, as well as a chance for Scotland to beat the tourists for the first time. Could Scotland do it?

As the play developed, Scotland became engaged in more defensive than attacking work, and while new cap Andy Irvine performed brilliantly at full back and Ian McGeechan did some good clearing work, it was the All Blacks who did most of the attacking to enjoy the territorial advantage. Yet they were not inspired and Scotland were able to keep their line intact. No further kicks at goal presented themselves to Karam, despite the fact that the French referee, Georges Domercq maintained a close 'surveillance' on the proceedings.

Injury time was entered after 40 minutes of the first-half without any score and then suddenly the Scottish defence broke down outside its own line on the blind side. The All Blacks won a scrum, Going went away towards the open, changed to the blind, was tackled and Wyllie took the pass and moved inside flanker MacEwan, who was partially obstructed, to fall over the line before No. 8 Peter Brown could get up to tackle him.

Karam converted this try and the All Blacks changed ends with a valuable six points. lead. The attacking scrum position had been achieved as the result of a long run by Bryan Williams down the right wing, following a break by Going. Williams was stopped by the new wing, David Sheddan, but the scrum 10 yards out set it up for New Zealand, who were always happier moving the ball from the scrum or ruck inside their opponents 25, especially to the blind side, or kicking over the forwards. It was Going's kick over the forwards on the Welsh '25' at Cardiff that led to the try by Murdoch, after Bevan and John Williams failed to clear.

After four minutes of the second-half, Irvine had cut the All Blacks' lead by half with an excellent 35-yard penalty goal and the match was alive. There had been some speculation during the interval when Robertson went to the touch-line, asking to come off. Hurst, his possible replacement, was there, limbering up, but the duty M.O. and specialist refused to grant permission for the replacing of Robertson.

It was fortunate for the All Blacks that they made this decision, because Robertson laid on the second try for his side after 18 minutes of the second-half. The All Blacks won a line-out and Robertson switched play back to the right, breaking through tackles and then grub-kicking back to the left, where the Scottish line was unguarded. Batty chased for the ball as it rolled over the line and Steele, drawn in to cover the Robertson break, turned and raced back, but was just beaten for the touch down.

So it was 10–3 to New Zealand, but five minutes later McGeechan dropped a neat left-footed goal for Scotland after receiving from a line-out to make it 10–6. Soon afterwards, Irvine landed a beautiful 54-yard penalty and it was 10–9. Now anybody's game, and with a try at three points and a dropped goal at four, it would have been 10–9 to Scotland!

Still, New Zealand, with two tries, deserved their lead, but the final fifteen minutes, including five of injury time, proved the best and most exciting of the match. Scotland tried desperately hard to snatch the match out of the fire, but New Zealand were not going to concede such a valuable prize. They defended, counter attacked, defended and waited since Scotland had made errors in attacking positions. They would make another, possibly, and they did. This time in the fifth and final minute of injury time, near the half-way line when trying desperately to launch a final attack. A blind pass from lock McHarg to Steele was snapped up by Going with a clever interception. Scotland were caught – all up in attack – and away went Going – 55 yards for the line – and a deserved try in the corner. Batty got inside Going, so the try was never in doubt, and it mattered little that Karam could not convert it.

The final whistle went; it was all over, with New Zealand as deserving winners, and looking better all-round as a side, although the match was never as pulsating as the Welsh match. Scotland did not prove powerful enough at forward and allowed the All Blacks too much possession, conceding to them the initiative in attack. Thus it was New Zealand who put more pressure on Scotland than the Scots could put upon the All Blacks.

Scotland made many errors, and indeed the All Blacks seem to win more matches on opponents' errors than by their own creative ability. However, if they win enough possession they can kick, drive and ruck, to force their opponents into errors. Bravely though Scotland played, they had to give best on the day to New Zealand, who stood two up with two to play in the Tests. This was a comfortable position, much more so than was anticipated at the start of the tour!

9 *Lost in the Fog*

After the Scottish match Bob Duff was pleased and commented, 'Both individually and collectively we exercised more control than against Wales, but, of course, a team ought to improve as a tour goes along.' Ian Kirkpatrick looked ahead to the three remaining Tests and said, 'If we play as well in the internationals to come, as we did against Scotland, I am sure we can do it.'

Before the Scottish match, it was reported that Ernie Todd had motivated the team by emphasising the point that no All Blacks side had won all five Tests on a European tour. The unbeaten 1924–25 side did not meet Scotland and the 1967 side did not visit Ireland. 'I hoped,' said Todd, 'it would give them the incentive to play just that little harder, and perhaps it did.'

Scotland did not play as well as anticipated and the All Blacks did rather better behind than in previous matches. The match was decided simply by New Zealand's superior forward play which enabled them to put pressure on the Scottish halves and backs in general.

Before the next match of the tour, at Oxford on December 20 against the Southern Counties, the England selectors announced their side to oppose the All Blacks at Twickenham on January 6. This contained only one new cap in the 21-year-old student, Peter Warfield, in the centre. He had played extremely well for the North Eastern Counties at Bradford and was a splendid tackler. The rest of the side was based on the successful tour party that visited South Africa earlier in the year, with the addition of Lion David Duckham. Many of the players selected had already played against the tourists with success for their provincial sides. John Pullin was named as captain, but most critics felt that the omission of Peter Dixon on the flank was a major error. He was bigger than Watkins and Neary for the end of the line-out, and had appeared in three of the four 1971 Tests.

In the New Zealand camp there was concern over the serious injury to prop Jeff Matheson, who could not remember how it happened. He remained behind in hospital in Edinburgh in considerable pain, while the management waited patiently in the hope that he would be able to play again. Gordon Rowley told me that 'sprung ribs' would take at least six weeks to mend, and this ruled out the remainder of the British section of the tour. Thus it was inevitable that the injured prop would have to be replaced and, eventually, on Boxing Day, it was announced that 'Sandy' McNicol of Wanganui, would fly here to replace the unfortunate Matheson. A strange coincidence, as the Lions lost two props in 1971 – though by slightly different methods from those which caused the departure of Murdoch and Matheson! The end of the year was approaching and there was still no news of Murdoch, who had really 'gone to ground', somewhere in Australia.

The Southern Counties made no pretence to greatness, but, nevertheless, were full of spirit and determination. Several members of the team could not command regular places in their club sides, and this was true of their captain, John Vaughan of the London Welsh. Lindsay Clark, the replacement for Murdoch, made his début at prop while Ted Howard, the team secretary, left for London, having been ordered to rest, following over-work. A Welshman, C. G. P. Thomas, was the referee in charge, while a former captain of Oxford University, Owen Jones, was in the centre. Conditions were good but cold, and a crowd of five thousand at Iffley Road during University vacation, represented good support for a match the All Blacks were 'certain' of winning.

Eighteenth Match
Versus Southern Counties at Oxford, December 20.
New Zealand won by two goals, one penalty goal and two tries (23) to one goal (6).
Weather: Dry and cold. *Ground:* Firm. *Crowd:* 5,000.
TEAMS:
SOUTHERN COUNTIES: S. Crabtree (*Bristol*); R. Ellis Jones (*London Welsh*), R. O. P. Jones (*Oxford*), I. Ray (*Oxford*), P. Cadle (*Saracens*); D. Llewellyn (*London Welsh*), D.

Spawforth (*Army*); M. R. Hannell (*Bristol*), H. Malins (*Richmond*), K. Richardson (*Gloucester*), J. S. Jarrett (*Gloucester*), J. Harwood (*Oxford*), M. Marshall (*Richmond*), S. Godfrey (*Loughborough Colleges*), J. Vaughan (*London Welsh,* capt.).

NEW ZEALAND: T. J. Morris; B. G. Williams, I. A. Hurst, M. Sayers, D. A. Hales; I. N. Stevens, G. L. Colling; G. J. Whiting, R. A. Urlich, L. Clark, A. M. Haden, I. M. Eliason, K. W. Stewart, B. E. Holmes, I. A. Kirkpatrick (capt.).

Referee: C. G. P. Thomas (Wales).

The All Blacks did win, as expected, by 23 points to six, but again they did not impress. They should have won by at least 40 points, even though the Counties put up a brave display. Manager Todd was forthright and accurate, 'One or two sparkling things, a lot of indifferent play, but not the sort of performance anyone is going to remember.'

Pat Marshall, in the *Daily Express*, wrote, 'I think it was the poorest display I've seen by any All Blacks side. The score, considering the possession won, should have been in the upper forties.' Barry John, in the same paper, wrote, 'Their passing was dreadful and it seemed at times that Stevens, Hurst and Sayers were deliberately trying to set each other up for the tackle. Six consecutive rucks were won at one time, but no try ever looked like materialising.' Even Terry McLean cabled that it was tiresome that so much effort yielded so little.

To say the least, it was uninspiring and disappointing, and did nothing to suggest that the tourists were improving. The forwards were bigger and heavier and won the line-outs by three to one, and the rucks by six to one. The ball was constantly in the hands of scrum-half Lyn Colling, and while he gave his backs a reasonable share of it, he also tried to play in the Going manner. It is always a mistake for a player to attempt to change his style in mid-tour. He may have been obeying instructions, but I preferred to watch the true Colling of Otago, rather than a not-so-successful imitation of Going of North Auckland.

Again, poor Trevor Morris at full-back was out of touch as a place kicker, missing goals that he would have kicked with ease in New Zealand. What agony this likeable fellow must have gone through, yet success was just round the corner for him, but would it be permanent? Of the team's leading players, he was the unluckiest, recalling the misfortunes of Stewart Wilson, the 1966 Lion in New Zealand.

In the first half, it took the All Blacks 32 minutes to register their first score and at half-time it was only 11–0 with two tries by Williams and Hales and a penalty by Morris. After the interval, Williams got a second try, converted by Morris from the touch-line, followed by one from the big lock, Haden, which Morris converted. This was the end of the All Blacks' scoring and the Counties finished strongly, as left wing Cadle intercepted to get a try at the posts which Llewellyn converted. The match was over and we left Oxford for home and Christmas, almost wondering if the All Blacks just rucked for the sake of it, and not as a scoring exercise!

The All Blacks returned to London for Christmas and enjoyed a few days well-deserved rest in the big city. The players were told before they left Oxford who would be required for the Boxing Day match against the Combined Services and the rest were able to relax. However, the redoubtable 'Grizz' Wyllie took several players for a training spin in Hyde Park on the Sunday morning and there were half a dozen who actually went to the park on Christmas morning! Each player was allowed two days food allowance of £10 in case they wanted to eat out in London.

All this appeared to contradict the criticism of Bob Duff's so-called 'barbaric' training methods, which had been cabled home by New Zealand correspondents. Actually, the players enjoyed training and Duff's alleged '25 years old' coaching and training methods were bringing results in the shape of consecutive victories, as the side settled down to a steady routine. By this time officials and followers had accepted them for what they were, and there was a temporary truce in the 'charge and counter charge' process.

The Combined Services match brought to light again the 'forgotten man' of British rugby, Mike Campbell-Lamerton, who had led the ill-fated 1966 Lions with intense dedication and lost two stones in weight in the process. He was given the task of coaching the Combined Services and bringing the three Services into line as a team and provide the All Blacks with reasonable opposition.

The Combined Services included five international players in

Turk, Steele and Clarke of Scotland, Larter of England, and Young of Wales, who was elected captain. The scrum-half, Corporal Spawforth, had played on the previous Wednesday at Oxford and the side looked good enough to test the tourists, who included eleven players who had appeared in Test matches which included eleven players who had appeared in Test matches during or before the tour. Wyllie was the acting captain, as both Kirkpatrick and Going were resting, and there were hopes that Morris and Burgess would enjoy a return to their best form.

Nineteenth Match
Versus Combined Services at Twickenham, December 26.
New Zealand won by two goals, four penalty goals, one dropped goal and one try (31) to two penalty goals and one try (10).
Weather: Dry and cold. *Ground:* Firm. *Crowd:* 15,000.
TEAMS:
COMBINED SERVICES: Tpr. A. S. Turk (*Army*); Cpl. W. C. Steele (*RAF*), Capt. D. S. Boyle (*Army*), 2nd/Lt. P. M. Davies (*Army*), Sub/Lt. G. P. Phillips (*Navy*); P/O. G. Jones (*Navy*), Cpl. D. Spawforth (*Army*); R.E.A. J. C. Ackerman (*Navy*), Inst.Lt. R. L. Clarke (*Navy*), Flt./Lt. J. Young (*RAF*, capt.), F/Off. P. J. Larter (*RAF*), Sgt. I Cairns (*Army*), Lt. A. J. W. Higginson (*Marines*), Sgt. P. Warder (*RAF*), Lt. P. J. Bird (*Army*). *Replacement:* Cpl. D. R. Pulford (*RM*) for Ackerman.
NEW ZEALAND: T. J. Morris; G. B. Batty, I. A. Hurst, R. M. Parkinson, G. R. Skudder; R. E. Burgess, G. L. Colling; L. Clark, R. A. Urlich, K. K. Lambert, P. J. Whiting, I. M. Eliason, A. J. Wyllie (capt.), B. Holmes, A. I. Scown.
Referee: N. P. Jones (Gloucestershire).

This match was won in the manner of so many others, through good work by the pack and successful place kicking. The return to form of Trevor Morris was most welcome for this hitherto uncertain full-back, with a remarkable reputation as a place kicker, had failed to do himself justice. This time he collected 19 points with seven goal kicks to achieve the top individual match score of the tour and pass Joe Karam's total of 15 against Wales.

Morris played so much better that it was good to see him enjoying himself, and he punished numerous errors by the

England's David Duckham, out on his own and about to be tackled by Grant Batty. The England backs never received enough good ball to realise their potential

The 'wrestling match' in the game against Newport: Bryan Williams tries to prise apart Peter Whiting and Lyn Jones as referee Larry Lamb hurries to the scene

Against Midland Counties East and Neath/Aberavon, the All Blacks showed what they were capable of when they were allowed to run. *Above:* Ian Kirkpatrick and his forwards dominated the line-outs against Midlands East and (*below*) Bob Burgess crosses the Neath/Aberavon line to score the first of his two tries

Services in the process. For 35 of the 45 minutes allowed for the first half, the Services held out, but then conceded two penalties and a dropped goal by Morris plus a 'gift' try by Batty. The All Blacks were 13 points ahead at the interval and in no danger of defeat, but the Services had 'allowed' them rather than their being created.

Morris's dropped goal was a beauty and its artistry not only impressed one, but substantiated the claim that, on his day, he was a fine Test player. The refereeing did not impress me as Mr Jones of Gloucester appeared to miss far too many technical infringements and allow the All Blacks considerable latitude at the line-out. He was not always up with the play, as when the Services scored their try, and the All Blacks got one by Scown.

Where the All Blacks really failed in this match, of which they always had the winning, was in not running the ball more readily. Wyllie, as captain, drove his forwards hard enough, but did not get his backs to run, and a gifted attacker like Burgess spent most of the afternoon kicking. It was a day for celebration and one would have preferred the gayer approach of Manchester's men of 1935, or the 1945 Kiwis, who would have enjoyed their Boxing Day!

In the second half, Peter Larter kicked two fifty-yard penalty goals for the Services and Peter Davies, son of a former Welsh international centre, got an individualist try for the Services. Mike Parkinson and Alistair Scown scored tries for the All Blacks which Trevor Morris converted, as well as kicking two penalty goals.

The All Blacks had an 'evening out' with the Services but did not stay long and then a day's rest in London on Wednesday. I spent the day at Chessington Zoo with my grandchildren and returned to Cardiff the next day after a change of scenery that was interesting. At least one could forget the rigours of the tour and all the millions of words written by rugby writers and commentators. Yet one did wonder where Keith Murdoch was 'hiding' and, on return to Cardiff, I received an airmail from Jack Manchester of Dunedin, who was sad the Murdoch incident had occurred, but not surprised!

The East Glamorgan team had a good work out on the Thursday afternoon and reported fit under coach Leighton Davies, who hit out at the 'knockers' that the match was just a

I

'sop' and his team would be over-run by the All Blacks. When asked if they would score 30 points against his side, Davies, a tough little former wing-forward and P.E. lecturer, answered, 'That's rubbish!'

I visited Ernie Todd, Bob Duff and Handel Rogers at the Angel Hotel and chatted to them over a few beers. It is not part of my professional approach to continually 'chase' tour managers, but an occasional meeting does keep one in touch and if any article has been misinterpreted, it can be put right. Yet this was not one of those occasions, and Ernie Todd spoke of his meeting with Peter Hein, of the future of Springbok rugby and the 1973 tour in New Zealand.

The All Blacks had nominated an extremely strong XV to oppose East Glamorgan and Todd said this was a tribute to Welsh rugby as a whole. 'We always rate Welsh opposition as the best we shall meet on tour. Many tell us that East Glamorgan will not be as strong as some other sides met in Wales, but we are not taking any chances. We are fielding a good side and are looking forward to an interesting game.'

Todd confessed to enjoying his return to Cardiff and did not recall any details of the Murdoch incident. Duff said he enjoyed his training sessions and, contrary to belief, so did the players. 'They'll go out voluntarily if I don't arrange a session, and several of them really enjoyed running in Hyde Park on Christmas morning! You cannot argue about that!'

Twentieth Match
Versus East Glamorgan at Cardiff Arms Park, December 30.
New Zealand won by one goal, two penalty goals and two tries (20) to two penalty goals and one dropped goal (9).
Weather: Dense fog. *Ground:* Good. *Crowd:* 25,000.
TEAMS:
EAST GLAMORGAN: C. Bolderson (Pontypridd); D. Schick (*Bridgend*), I. Hopkins (*Cardiff College of Education*), I. Hall (*South Wales Police*), V. Jenkins (*Bridgend*); R. Evans and G. Evans (*South Wales Police*); D. J. Lloyd (*Bridgend*, capt.), C. Lewis (*Glamorgan Wanderers*), A. Davies (*South Wales Police*), W. Howe (*Maesteg*), P. Williams (*Bridgend*), R. Dudley-Jones (*Cardiff College of Education*), D. Brain (*Bridgend*), G. Jones (*Bridgend*). *Replacement:* D. John (*Pontypridd*) for G. Evans.
NEW ZEALAND: J. F. Karam; B. G. Williams, I. A. Hurst,

B. J. Robertson, D. A. Hales; I. N. Stevens, S. M. Going; K. K. Lambert, R. W. Norton, G. J. Whiting, P. J. Whiting, H. H. Macdonald, I. A. Kirkpatrick (capt.), A. R. Sutherland, B. Holmes. *Replacement:* L. A. Clark for G. J. Whiting.

Referee: K. H. Clark (Ireland).

This was a remarkable match in every way: the most unusual of the tour. It was nearly called off before it started because the City of Cardiff was visited by a dense fog on the day, which shrouded the historic Cardiff Arms Park. W.R.U. secretary Bill Clement rang me at home, early in the morning, about replacement Lindsay Clark, and announced, 'You cannot see one side of the Park from the other. The match may be off!' The River Taff runs along the west end of the Arms Park and this water encouraged the fog, wafting thick clouds of damp mist down along the ground and swirling into the high stands.

W.R.U. treasurer, Kenneth Harris, and committee man Les Spence, conferred with Bill Clement while coach organiser Ray Williams made continual inspections of the ground from different positions to test visibility. The All Blacks management and captain were called in but, as time was moving on past noon, a decision had to be made. Both teams wanted to play and Irish referee, Kenneth Clark, said he would agree to play and continue playing, as long as he could keep the flight of the ball in vision. It was agreed to play!

The Police and stewards were informed and the gates opened with suitable notices posted and the public advised by loud hailer that no play or 'Vision' could be guaranteed! This was an understatement, for when the teams fielded it was still dense enough to prevent an overall view from the Press box or the stands. The officials had been influenced by a weather report indicating that the fog would ease, and also by the other two factors that the match, if cancelled, could not have been replayed during the tour, and that all the players were anxious to play.

I am sure they enjoyed it for most of the time and East Glamorgan put up a brave showing, after it had been suggested that they would lose by twenty to thirty points. Only one incident marred the whole proceedings and this was witnessed from the press box and by most spectators in the South Stand.

It occurred after 30 minutes of the second half. Going was

penalised for obstruction on Ron Evans, the East Glamorgan outside-half, after he had kicked ahead. Going appeared to pause at the scene and Derek Brain, a Glamorgan forward, pushed him away, in the back. Another forward was at hand and Going turned with his fists at the 'ready'. The Glamorgan scrum-half, Gareth Evans, trotted up to the scene as a 'peace-maker', but he was felled with two punches, one-two, that would have done credit to Bob Foreman!

Evans was out 'cold' with his lip split right through to his teeth below his nose, and had to be 'escorted' from the field bleeding profusely. The referee saw it all happen, and called Going to one side and started writing in his notebook while the crowd yelled, 'Off, off!' It was a nasty incident and as the crowd booed, poor N.Z.B.C. commentator, Bob Irvine could only say, 'They're booing again in Wales. They always boo in Wales!'

The W.R.U. officials and N.Z. party did not 'see' the incident as they were in the North Stand, the score at this stage being 16–9 to the All Blacks. Afterwards, Evans, following 15 stitches being inserted in his lip in hospital, commented, 'I was running after the ball when Going was penalised for obstruction. The next thing I knew, there was a fist coming from somewhere and it hit me twice. Then I was down on the ground. I put my hand to my mouth and found I had a handful of blood.' Evans, a Porthcawl policeman, added, 'I am not particularly upset, you have got to take the rough with the smooth in rugby.' His lot was a 'rough' one on this occasion!

Going could claim that he had been provoked by the push in the back, but did this justify action that sent Evans to hospital? Were British referees leaning over 'backwards' so as not to send an All Black off the field? Were the All Blacks taking advantage of the situation and why was the punching always at the Cardiff Arms Park?

The crowd booed Going until the end of the match and I felt he deserved the 'treatment' since, whatever the cause, he surely could not expect the crowd to ignore his action. Welshmen are generous in their praise of great players, especially New Zealanders, as the illustrious Wilson Whineray, will testify following his experience at the Arms Park in 1964. Had he been captain on this tour, things might have been different, because 'Kirky' did not appear to exercise full discipline on the field although, after this incident, he did speak for some time to Going.

The Sunday critics really had a 'go' and Ken Jones, 1950 British Lion, asked in the *Sunday Express*. 'Why was Going not ordered off?' Vivian Jenkins, 1938 Lion, was disturbed in the *Sunday Times*. Wilfred Wooller in the *Sunday Telegraph* said 'Going's punch deepens gloom' and went on sternly, 'Rugby is supposed to be an amateur game, played for fun. The Seventh All Blacks can lay claim to being the most unpopular touring side seen in these Islands.' Wooller, a noted official in World cricket, a writer on sport for 25 years and a brilliant big centre and match winner, who had played against Manchester's men in 1935, added, 'They were great fellows, on and off the field, but this side does not amuse or entertain me.'

Many of the remaining friends in the stand were lost by New Zealand in this match and, once again, they had 'dropped one' to add to their growing list of rather ungracious acts. The 'chip on the shoulder' was getting bigger. It was all so sad, for it could have been otherwise, had they chosen a different approach. The All Blacks did not appear to be making every effort to encourage rugby followers to like them, and Welshmen were most disappointed that the tour was not a completely happy one.

Even the Press could not claim to have seen ALL of the play. We did see one All Blacks try, the first, by Duncan Hales, after Colin Bolderson had put Glamorgan in the lead with a 35 yard penalty goal, followed by one from Joe Karam, a steady young full-back and a most pleasant, modest fellow. This made it seven points to three before Karam kicked his second penalty, followed by a thirty yard dropped goal from the 'veteran' outside-half Ron Evans, another policeman, to make the interval score, 10–6, which was much better than anticipated by the crowd.

Early in the second half, Ian Hopkins, from Cardiff College of Education, kicked a straight 30 yard penalty and it was 10–9. Surely, the impossible was not to happen? For 15 minutes the Welshman battled away before the decisive points came when Stevens scored—or was it Hales—from a kick ahead by the heavily bandaged Bruce Robertson. This try was converted and the All Blacks were safe again at 16–9. Before end, Hales got his second—or was it his third—try. Blast the fog, but the end came at 20–9 and a most creditable performance by the Men from the East, who were given no chance at all.

Bob Howitt, invited to give the New Zealand viewpoint in the *Western Mail* argued that Going had been provoked, in his piece on Monday morning, but added, 'What does concern me about the Going incident is that: (1) As the All Blacks vice-captain, he should never have stooped to such an action. (2) He could have been sent off and, if suspended, missed the England match. Remember it was Kevin Kelleher who sent Colin Meads from Murrayfield in 1967 for a seemingly less brutal offence than Going's . . . Let's face it, this All Blacks team without Going, is only half a team.'

Honest opinion . . . not 'one eyed'. It is good that Howitt was covering the tour, and 'seeing' both sides of the scene. Going was not helping himself or the image of the All Blacks.

10 *England, my England!*

The All Blacks left Cardiff for Penzance on the Sunday and if one had been a writer of crime stories one would have had to suggest that they were still the 'villains of the piece' and not the pin-up boys that people back home in the two Islands were led to believe! The Seventh All Blacks just could not endear themselves to the Welsh in the manner of their predecessors.

They announced that Jake Young, the Scottish referee who did not warn any player in the hectic match against the Cardiff club, would be the referee for the England Test. The next day they met the South Western Counties, a combined Cornwall and Devon side, at Redruth, and the referee, appointed and not invited, since the All Blacks only nominated referees for Test matches, was the dapper little Welshman, Ernie Lewis, of Abertillery, a former outside-half, and an official of considerable experience, known as a fair-minded trouble-shooter!

Trevor Morris was in the All Blacks' side at full-back and rapidly regaining form as a kicker while Alan Pearn, the Bristol scrum-half, was in the Counties side, and because Lewis was a strict referee, one anticipated a keen kicking duel between these two experts, if they were on form. Pearn was on the way to an individual record as a points scorer and so he, rather than Morris, held the key to the match.

Twenty-first Match
Versus South Western Counties at Redruth, January 2.
New Zealand won by one goal and six tries (30) to one penalty goal and one try (7).
Weather: Fine. *Ground:* Good. *Crowd:* 22,000
TEAMS:
SOUTH WESTERN COUNTIES: R. C. Staddon (Exeter); K. C. Plummer (Bristol), T. Palmer (Gloucester, capt.), R. Friend (Plymouth Albion), R. Warmington (St Luke's Col-

lege, Exeter); N. Bennett (St Luke's College, Exeter), A. Pearn (Bristol); D. Hosking (Hayle), J. Lockyear (Exeter), P. Baxter (Exeter), J. Scott (Exeter), J. Baxter (Exeter), A. Cole (Exeter), A. Hollins (Exeter), P. J. Hendy (St Ives).

NEW ZEALAND: T. J. Morris; D. A. Hales, I. A. Hurst, M. Sayers, G. B. Batty; R. E. Burgess, G. L. Colling; K. K. Lambert, R. A. Urlich, L. A. Clark, A. M. Haden, I. M. Eliason, K. W. Stewart, A. J. Wyllie, I. A. Kirkpatrick (capt.).

Referee: E. M. Lewis (Wales).

The All Blacks won comfortably in the end, by 30 points to seven, but Pearn was still the key to the match, for he missed eight out of nine reasonable attempts at goal. In the end, the Counties collapsed and the All Blacks ran with the ball against a weakening defence.

At the interval, the All Blacks led by a point, a try to a penalty goal, and the Counties were very much in the match. Another 12 minutes elapsed, and it was still 4–3, but then the normally accurate Pearn missed with three vital penalty attempts. Had they been kicked, the Counties could have been uplifted, as they were playing with real tearaway spirit. However, the All Blacks were once again let off the hook!

The tourists realised the match was there for the taking, since poor Alan Pearn, a modest fellow, was not going to kick any more goals during the afternoon. They went further ahead and swept through the Western Counties ranks like the forces of Cromwell and by no-side had won 30–7. Yet Morris was just as much off form as poor Pearn!

Referee Lewis was far from satisfied with the approach of the All Blacks. He watched obstruction at the line-out; he watched Wyllie running back from the line-out, and when Wyllie protested, he told Kirkpatrick to tell him to keep quiet. In all, he awarded 20 penalties against the All Blacks, nine of them in kickable positions, but he insisted, as he does in all his matches, on strict observation of the laws. Lewis is a rugger man, and he doesn't worry about size or reputation, and to him Wyllie was just another player, the same as the other 29, and not a coaxer of referees. At least, not on this day.

The All Blacks did not like Mr Lewis and made this obvious afterwards by ignoring him. However, one player made it especially clear that, in his opinion, Mr Lewis was lacking in his knowledge of the laws. When Mr Lewis asked him for his autograph afterwards, he replied in the negative in no uncertain manner, and made an impolite reference to Mr Lewis's lack of knowledge of the laws!

When Mr Lewis recalled the short, but rather abrasive reply to his request, at the end of the tour, he laughed, with his eyes twinkling – 'Funny fellows, those All Blacks. Quite unlike their previous sides. They just don't mix. I don't make the laws, either. They are in the law book and I interpret them.' Like Air Commodore Larry Lamb, who was to scrutinise the All Blacks' approach very closely at Newport, Lewis was a former panel referee and he stood no 'nonsense'. Had he been put in charge of a Ranfurly Shield match between Canterbury and Auckland, he would have been just as strict and he does not enjoy players telling him how to do his job! Refereeing is not an easy job at any time, but players can make it easier for officials if they get on with the game and do not dispute decisions. I recall another strict referee, Paddy d'Arcy, of Ireland, reportedly telling Colin Meads in 1967 – 'You get on with playing, Mr Meads, and I'll get on with refereeing!'

In his cable to the *New Zealand Herald,* Terry McLean had this to say: 'Sometimes, coincidentally, a referee from Wales did more than stir the All Blacks' blood. He often brought it to the boil . . . Mr Lewis was a touch judge at the ghostly affair which was the All Blacks' match against East Glamorgan. He will be most lastingly remembered among the eccentricities of Redruth.'

How the All Blacks – players and Press – loved the Welsh. The healthy rivalry was turning sour and the Welsh, with their intensity of purpose and genuine regard for New Zealand rugby, just could not understand these Seventh All Blacks. They put the question . . . 'How do you really get to know them?' It was answered by the young player who was quoted in the *New Zealand Herald* as saying, 'We have not come to Britain to make friends!' How sad . . . for them and for the game, and especially for the warm-hearted country of New Zealand.

For the All Blacks, Batty (3), Hurst (2), Burgess and Kirkpatrick scored tries and Kent Lambert, the prop, converted one of them after poor Trevor Morris had failed several times. Pearn kicked one penalty and Plummer got a try late in the match for the Counties, whose brave forward play deserved a better fate.

The All Blacks wasted many chances until they recovered their poise late in the match, when the large crowd gave them a big hand. That evening the tourists announced their side for the Twickenham Test, while England announced a change at prop. Fran Cotton dropped out through injury and was replaced by Frank Anderson of Orrell to give the Lancashire club its first cap; he earned it by his good display in the North Western's victory at Workington. The All Blacks' side erred on the side of caution, preferring Parkinson to Hurst, and refusing to reinstate Burgess in the Test side. Stevens, who replaced him as he did against Scotland, 'toed the party line' while Graham Whiting was selected and hoped to play, although his ear had proved most painful during the stay in Cornwall.

On the Thursday, an outstanding England forward of the 1920s died; Sam Tucker of Bristol, who made 27 appearances, including one against the 1924–25 All Blacks in the memorable match at Twickenham when the late and incomparable Cyril Brownlie was sent off before the Prince of Wales. Sam was the first rugby player to fly to an international match – from Bristol to Cardiff in 1930.

England believed they had a reasonable chance of victory, based on the team spirit developed in South Africa. John Pullin was a good captain and the side had resolution, but one was concerned at the comparatively small flank forwards, Watkins and Neary, and the lack of pace and, indeed, kicking form of big Sam Doble at full-back compared with his previous record-breaking seasons. Then, on the eve of the match, outside-half Alan Old aggravated a hamstring injury and an SOS was sent for John Finlan of Moseley to substitute and play with club-mate, Jan Webster.

Twenty-second Match
Versus England at Twickenham, January 6.
New Zealand won by one goal and one dropped goal (9) to nil.
Weather: Damp, cold. *Ground:* Slippery. *Crowd:* 72,000.
TEAMS:
ENGLAND: S. A. Doble (Moseley); A. J. Morley (Bristol), P. J. Warfield (Rosslyn Park), P. S. Preece (Coventry), D. J. Duckham (Coventry); J. F. Finlan (Moseley), J. G. Webster

(Moseley); C. B. Stevens (Penzance-Newlyn), J. V. Pullin (Bristol, capt.), W. F. Anderson (Orrell), C. W. Ralston (Richmond), P. J. Larter (Northampton), J. A. Watkins (Gloucester), A. G. Ripley (Rosslyn Park), A. Neary (Broughton Park).

NEW ZEALAND: J. F. Karam; B. G. Williams, B. J. Robertson, R. M. Parkinson, G. B. Batty; I. N. Stevens, S. M. Going; K. K. Lambert, R. W. Norton, G. J. Whiting, P. J. Whiting, H. H. Macdonald, A. J. Wyllie, A. R. Sutherland, I. A. Kirkpatrick (capt.).

Referee: J. Young (Scotland).

One of the flankers, Tony Neary, was passed fit to play with a hairline fracture of the right cheekbone, while the more experienced Peter Dixon, a British Lion of 1971, was left on the touch line. A mistake, one felt at the time, and after the match, which was won by New Zealand, deservedly. England wasted many a chance, while the All Blacks played it 'close to their chests', giving nothing away and pouncing on English errors. Sad, but a full exposé of the New Zealand approach – hard play at forward supported by the shrewd Going at scrum-half.

The high hopes of an England victory forecast by the *Daily Mail, Daily Mirror, Guardian* and John Dawes, were destroyed by the poor kicking form of Sam Doble, a possible error by Referee Young, who disallowed a try by England at a critical time in the game, and the good tight and loose play of the All Blacks' forwards. If the referee did make an error, as England's chairman of selectors, Sandy Sanders, believed, then it was the turning point in the match, but the New Zealanders did deserve their victory.

The England forwards put up a brave showing and should have earned a somewhat better fate, but the side as a whole made too many errors, and Sid Going was able to dictate in the first half, when the match was won and lost. Afterwards, England marked him more closely, but they ended as the first side of the tour not to register a score against the tourists.

When under pressure the All Blacks gambled in defence. Once, Grant Batty dashed in to take the inside centre with England shaping up for a 3 to 1 overlap. He spoiled the movement with his crashing tackle. Then, after the All Blacks had snatched an early six points lead, England could have equalised in the second half but Referee Young adjudged the scoring pass from Warfield to Preece was forward.

Almost immediately after this incident, Finlan was clearing under pressure from his own line and failed to find touch. Bryan Williams gathered 40 yards out and, from a wide angle, dropped a lovely high goal to make it 9–0 instead of a possible 6–6, and the match was over. For the remaining 20 minutes, the All Blacks played it cool and England could not recover. The tourists were now three Tests up with two to play!

Williams's goal was decisive, but it was the All Blacks' early score that really laid the foundation of victory, because once achieved (after six minutes) it required England to score twice, at least, to get ahead, and they failed. They had their chances, but the big kicking Sam Doble, hero of Ellis Park, fired wide and these were mortal blows to England's hopes.

The All Blacks' try was achieved by a long throw-in. Neary was pulled down at the end of the line when he should have been free to get at Going as the scrum-half gathered the ball. On went Going, to crash his way past Finlan and get well into the England '25' before slipping to Wyllie, who then handed on to Sutherland. He was tackled and from the ruck outside the England posts, New Zealand got the ball and Kirkpatrick dummied his way over for a try that Karam easily converted. England never really recovered from this early setback, which put them at a disadvantage throughout the match. Yet Doble could have retrieved much of it, had he kicked a couple of penalties, but 'ifs and buts' never won any match.

Carwyn James took up his pen for *The Observer* and commented, 'Dull, perhaps, but effective,' and ended his analysis with the following prophesy . . . 'Ireland and the Barbarians are now the only two international sides left which have a chance of beating the tourists. One feels it can still be done.' Yet he was shrewd enough to observe, 'One had the feeling, however, as so often on this tour, that the All Blacks had much in reserve. Their power up front was too much for the opposition.'

John Reed in the *Sunday Express* thought they would complete their tour unbeaten. John Reason, a stern critic of the New Zealanders throughout the tour, said in the *Daily Telegraph,* 'New Zealand's technique at the ruck and the maul was so infinitely superior that they won most of those that mattered.' Peter Wilson, out of retirement for the *Daily Mirror*, wrote, 'The giant New Zealand forwards proved that, in rugby at least, might IS right.' Barry John, in the *Daily Express*, praised England's pack, while Terry O'Connor, in the *Daily Mail*, devoted most of his report to the disallowed Preece try.

In the *Western Mail*, I wrote: 'They (All Blacks) believe rugby football is a game to be won without the open spectacle and appreciate that, even in this era of the amended laws, the well-placed high kick, ably followed up, and the ensuing speedy ruck, are just as effective as any spectacular threequarter move.'

For England it was a sad defeat, at a time when they felt they were on the upgrade. Their regional strength was not clearly revealed in the national XV and it was too early in the process of rehabilitation and reorganisation for them to succeed. The selectors had omitted better individual players for the sake of team spirit, but two points arose from the defeat.

First, the surface at Ellis Park in June was vastly different from that of Twickenham in January, and weight and strength was more important than the pace of the lighter men played. Secondly, the 1973 All Blacks were a much better and stronger side than the 1972 Springboks, disorganised by retirements and injuries that made six of their best players unavailable. England took their chance readily in June because Doble kicked the goals, but the situation was quite different in January and Doble did not kick any goals. It was not quite the Bing Crosby song, *When it's June in January*! It was not England's day, but they did try hard and it was a clean match!

11 *Return to Rodney Parade*

The word 'Newport' worries most touring sides to visit the British Isles, and the Rodney Parade ground in the Monmouthshire town even more so, since so many touring teams have been in trouble there since the war and, indeed, before that! The 1963–64 All Blacks and the 1969–70 Springboks suffered defeat there, while the 1960–61 Springboks, who won 3–0, were lucky to escape, as were the 1966–67 Wallabies with a 3–3 draw.

Further back, the 1945–46 Kiwis drew there 3–3; the 1953–54 All Blacks won 11–6; the 1924–25 Invincible All Blacks just got home 13–10 in the closing minutes, and Dave Gallaher's men just got home 6–3, but the 1912 Springboks lost 9–3. So this proud record produces a sense of apprehension in any touring team and, even though Newport were suffering one of their worst seasons for many years, the All Blacks still feared this Welsh club, that enjoys membership of both the RFU and the WRU.

They selected a strong XV to meet Newport, led by Sid Going, with 12 players who had appeared in Test rugby. Newport had to struggle to field a side, beset as they were by a crop of injuries to many senior and key players. They had only one international on view in No. 8 John Jeffery, who had appeared for Wales against New Zealand at Cardiff in 1967, and he, too, was just recovering from injury.

Yet the team had been well prepared by coaches Brian Jones and Ian McJennett, two former players who had much experience of 'battles' against touring teams – Jones had been a member of the 1961 Barbarians who defeated the Springboks. With the aid of my colleague Brian Wall, of the *South Wales Echo*, they had written an interesting book, *Rugby Under Pressure*, and few had made a closer study of the New Zealand approach, especially that of the Seventh All Blacks. They were not to be disappointed in the efforts of their team.

Twenty-third Match
Versus Newport at Rodney Parade, January 10.
New Zealand won by four penalty goals and two tries (20) to one goal, two penalty goals and one dropped goal (15).
Weather: Fine. *Ground:* Good. *Crowd:* 20,000.
TEAMS:
NEWPORT: R. J. Williams; G. Fuller, G. Talbot, N. Edwards, P. Ward; D. Rogers, A. Evans; I. Barnard, G. Williams, B. Rowland, L. Jones, J. Watkins, P. Watts, J. J. Jeffery, G. Evans (capt.).
NEW ZEALAND: T. J. Morris; B. G. Williams, B. J. Robertson, M. Sayers, G. R. Skudder; R. E. Burgess, S. M. Going (capt.); G. J. Whiting, R. A. Urlich, S. McNicol, P. J. Whiting, I. M. Eliason, A. I. Scown, B. Holmes, A. J. Wyllie.
Referee: Air Commodore G. C. Lamb (England).

The match began at a cracking pace with Newport tearing down to the right corner outside the All Blacks line and testing the touring team's defence. They were shaken and reminded, immediately, of the start at Llanelli. Once again, they had a real match on their hands. They were in Wales where, in the words of some of their less experienced rugby writers, 'Rugby is War!' A sad commentary upon their standard of observation and their background knowledge of the game throughout the world. It is dangerous to be so explicit, without true knowledge of the Welsh and their game, or indeed of any country!

Peter Whiting conceded the first penalty goal of the match and the second penalty kick to Newport, for barging at the line-out. Right-footed Robin Williams landed a lovely goal from the left-hand touch line. Three minutes later the first All Blacks penalty award, for offside at a ruck, saw Trevor Morris land a good 27 yard goal. These kicks suggested it would be a penalty duel between two fine kickers, and three minutes elapsed before Morris kicked his second goal from the same distance.

Referee Lamb was quick to spot this infringement and another, immediately afterwards, when Lyn Jones was the wrong side of a maul. This time, Morris kicked wide from the same distance and when Jones was struck in the face to draw blood, or 'Claret' as Terry McLean saw it, the game was stopped. Jones soon resumed and Going was penalised for the first time for 'not straight' at a scrum. There were cheers and the crowd felt that, here at last, was a referee who would blow for Super Sid's 'misdemeanours'. When he was penalised again, Robin Williams fired away at the posts from the half-way line and was near the target. He had another attempt, and this time the ball shaved the left upright. Morris tried from 45 yards when Newport were trapped, standing offside at a ruck but he was wide again.

After 30 minutes play there was a penalty kick for Newport at a scrum punch up and, from the right-hand touch line, on the '25', Williams kicked his second penalty for Newport, left-footed. The wonder boy, who did so well for Gwent in 1969 against the Springboks, was at it again. Morris had another kick from 35 yards from a Newport scrum infringement but was wide again.

It was six-all at half time, and the team without a chance had startled the rugby world. It was difficult to believe they had done so well but the second half was to prove even more illuminating. It was all action from the restart and first, when Newport were penalised at a line-out, new kicker Bryan Williams put over a splendid goal from 35 yards and the All Blacks were in the lead again at 9–6.

This score cheered them but the forward battle warmed to the boil and Super Sid was penalised for the third time for 'not straight' and the player asked the Referee . . . 'Give us a break, Ref?' to which the Referee replied, 'I will if you put the ball in correctly!'

Then Sid made a clever break up field and there was a fierce ruck with everything in. Back came the ball at speed and the All Blacks were away to the left, to reach wing George Skudder. He was checked by Robin Williams but managed to get the ball inside to Mark Sayers, who did well to get over the line. Bryan Williams' conversion attempt sailed wide but, ten minutes later, Newport were penalised for not releasing the ball in a tackle and Bryan Williams landed a 35 yard goal to make it 16–6, and for most people, the game was all over.

At least, to all except the fifteen Newport players. They were far from finished. In the 18 remaining minutes of play,

The Irish XV that drew with the All Blacks 10-10. Standing (*left to right*): K. Kelleher (touch judge), J. F. Slattery, T. O. Grace, T. A. P. Moore, K. M. A. Mays, W. J. McBride, J. J. Maloney, M. Joseph (referee), T. B. Kearns (touch judge); sitting: J. C. Davidson, K. W. Kennedy, C. M. H. Gibson, T. J. Kiernan (capt.), M. K. Flynn, J. F. Lynch, R. J. McLoughlin; in front: B. J. McGann and A. W. McMaster

Fergus Slattery (6), the Irish flanker, peels away as Ireland win a line-out

At last! The All Blacks perform the Haka before the start of the Barbarian match at Cardiff, the only time they did it on the tour. They appear to be enjoying it – the crowd certainly did

including injury time, the All Blacks did score again, but Newport collected nine points and rattled the tourists as had their illustrious predecessors wearing the famous black and amber jerseys. Newport threw in a long ball, over the top, at a line-out, but the All Blacks gathered and Sayers tried to kick clear from near his own line. Robin Williams fielded and dropped a quick goal from 25 yards. Then he was just short with a penalty attempt from 58 yards!

The match was decided, however, when for once the Newport halves dithered and Robertson intercepted, ran and handed on to Burgess who threw a long pass, slightly forward, since Bryan Williams had to turn back to take it, but the Referee was unsighted. On went Williams like the wind, to the corner and it was 20–9; no chance for Newport now. Yet back they came again, in the first minute of injury time, right from the restart after Williams' try. Edwards intercepted and raced away and although he probably would have got over on his own, he slipped the ball to hooker Gerwyn Williams, who was 'downed' short of the All Blacks line. Jeff Watkins was up to gather and dive over near the posts and Robin Williams had no difficulty in converting to make it 20–15. Could Newport achieve what was thought to be the 'impossible'?

New Zealand took a tight head scrum at a critical moment and soon the final whistle went and the crowd surged on to the field. Geoffrey Evans was proud of his team but the All Blacks left the field as 'silent men'. Only Burgess, always a gentleman. thanked the Referee for the game. Back in the dressing room after talking to Going, Manager Ernie Todd 'blew his top'. Sad but true, and the war of words was on again. These Welshmen . . . why didn't they allow the All Blacks to win easily. Why was it always so hard in Wales? The 'War' was on again!

Manager Todd accused the Referee of 'gunning' for poor Sid and this was an extremely childish comment. 'Sid was very nearly crying' said Todd. 'He felt the referee was gunning for him. At one stage of the match, when a scrum went down on the 25 yard line, Going said to the Referee, 'I am going to roll the ball in along this line.'

'He did so. But he was still penalised for allegedly putting the ball in crookedly. Going may give the impression of being off hand, or distant. In fact, he is extremely sensitive. He has come to feel very deeply that critics and referees are showing little or no understanding of what actually goes on when he puts the ball in. (Only New Zealanders know the procedure.)

'What is being overlooked is that, as Going lets the ball go from his hands, the loose head prop gives the signal for all out thrust by the pack. The object, naturally enough, is to push the opposing pack back far enough to give our hooker a fair go at the strike.'

If Mr Todd believed we would accept this argument, then he gave British rugby men little credit. He expected us to believe that Law 20 could be adjusted to suit New Zealand and especially Sid Going's requirements. Poor Super Sid was in trouble again during the Irish match for 'not straight', and one cannot accept the fact that most British referees were wrong and only Sid right. As for the lack of understanding, British referees never make a practice of favouring one player more than another, although one must accept the criticism that a few tend to be far too lenient with overseas players.

The match had another incident when, following a line-out, Lyn Jones of Newport and Peter Whiting were left wrestling on the ground. Play had moved over to the far side of the field while the 'unarmed combat' proceeded in front of the Press Box. Referee Lamb watched the play on the far side of the field and eventually awarded a penalty to N.Z. for a technical infringement.

Only then did he turn round to see what was happening and, by this time, the two offending players were locked in each others arms and quite unable to strike each other. Thus the Referee DID NOT SEE a blow being struck. Players of both teams helped Larry Lamb to prise the players apart and when they got up he lectured them 'good and proper', as real defaulters with a final warning.

He could do no more at that stage BECAUSE he did not see the punching and, in fairness to ALL referees, they can blow only for what they actually observe, and act accordingly. Had he seen the whole 'bout' then he may have acted quite differently but, as a critic that does not tolerate dirty play in any country, I felt that Larry Lamb was deserving of sympathy rather than blame in this instance. No referee should ever allow the crowd or the press to influence him.

The 'bout' made the headlines everywhere and my own

paper, the *Western Mail* had what I believe to have been an exclusive film strip of it. This was passed on to Thomson House, London, where it was distributed to several papers. In the *South Wales Argus* on the evening of the match, Sports Editor, Willis Huntley, an experienced journalist, gave Peter Whiting some 'stick' because he refused to shake the hand of rival Lyn Jones, who had extended it in friendship after the Referee's lecture. This insensed Mr Huntley who regarded it as 'one of the most unsporting acts ever witnessed at Rodney Parade.' He has watched international sport, rugby, soccer, tennis and cricket for 40 years, and he was not treating the matter lightly or looking for sensationalism.

Thus one's attention was drawn to the old parody, 'Although they liked the rugby, the fighting was the best!' – yet it WAS NOT a dirty match. There were few harder on the tour but only isolated incidents occurred that needed strict attention, and one could not understand what John Brooks, the N.Z.P.A. man was reporting when he said, 'It was a vicious brawling game before 22,000 spectators with their blood lust up.' A little exaggerated but then Mr Brooks came from Christchurch, the home of Canterbury rugby!

Unfortunately, the feuding did not end when the players left the field. The All Blacks did not shake hands 'all round' but went off to the hotel for their customary drink together before returning to Rodney Parade for the traditional dinner and dance. All went reasonably well until the 'incident' occurred, and nothing was publicised about this until Manager Todd held a press conference on the following Friday afternoon at the team's Leicester hotel, which was attended only by N.Z. Pressmen, not that others would have been refused entry.

It should be explained here that touring teams to the British Isles are never followed everywhere by the British press, as are British Teams in New Zealand, South Africa and Australia. Down under, the home press 'live' with the touring team but visiting teams to the British Isles enjoy far great privacy and can feed what they wish to their own press. This has never bothered me, and while in New Zealand they will have a press conference at the 'drop of a hat', there are rarely more than three or four official ones during a British tour.

One recalls after the Colin Meads 'incident' in 1967–68 that the N.Z. Pressmen had the full story 'in private from their management' but nothing was released to the British Press. Yet in fairness, it must be said that Managers Ernie Todd and Bob Duff on this tour was always approachable to the British Press and I was treated with every courtesy if I made a press enquiry. It is just that the Press, apart from the 'newshounds' on the Murdoch story, left them to enjoy their privacy.

The 'incident' involved All Blacks prop, Graham Whiting, and a Newport player not participating in the match, prop Gary Sutton. It appears that Graham Whiting was 'butted' in the face by Sutton but here are the two points of view. First Mr Todd, giving the N.Z. viewpoint . . . 'The incident occurred after the Newport player had "demanded" an autograph from Whiting, who asked him to wait. Next thing, Whiting was butted in the face and suffered a chipped tooth.'

Whiting momentarily stunned was seized by a team mate who said, 'Let's get out of here,' and they returned to their hotel. Mr Todd told the N.Z. Pressmen that he was writing to the Newport Club for a report of the 'incident' but informed that he had received an apology later in the evening from a club official.

The Newport player, Gary Sutton, had this to say, 'I asked Whiting for his autograph for my young sister and he signed the book. Then I asked him to pass it to another All Black but Whiting said, 'Say please.' I said, 'Oh come off it, Gary.' He just shook his head and threw the pen away. I told him to pick it up and he said something to me that I will not repeat. I hit him, he hit me; I hit him again, and then the fight was broken up. There was not really that much to it.'

Then Sutton added, when interviewed early on the Saturday morning, by a *Western Mail* news reporter, 'I don't want to say too much about the incident until I've had a word with club officials. But I was provoked and I have three witnesses to prove it. I cannot really see what all the fuss is about; after the fight was broken up, Graham went off and I didn't see him again. As far as I was concerned the incident was over and done with.'

There the matter ended. Newport received no official complaint in writing from the N.Z. management and, as it appeared to be 'half a dozen of one and six of the other', no one bothered to pursue it. What good would it have done? The All Blacks were never forthcoming to meet autograph requests anyway, and refused far more than they signed. There will come a day when no one will bother to ask them!

When I was a boy, and Jack Hobbs was the greatest name in cricket, he used to get a chair after lunch, light his pipe and sign one hundred books at a time, at Cardiff Arms Park. This was before Bradman, and I feel there is a lesson here... the greater the sportsman, the more ready he is to sign. None of the All Blacks could argue they were superior to Jack Hobbs!

12 *Across the Sea to Ireland*

The twenty-fourth match of the tour was at Leicester, on the historic ground at Welford Road, where internationals were played some fifty years ago. The East Midlands side had worked hard on their preparations, with a selection committee having first discussed the match as far back as August, 1972. A former England player and coach, Don White, had charge of the team and even though, when selected it contained only two England players in David Powell and Peter Larter, it was thought capable of giving the All Blacks a good, hard match.

The form of the Leicester Club, which supplied seven members of the combined team, had been rather 'in and out' through the first half of the season, but Northampton had five members in action, and there was also the most promising of young English forwards, Bob Wilkinson, in the second row with Larter. Yet the All Blacks still started as favourites.

They fielded a running side, pairing Burgess and Colling at half-back – players in the same mould, prepared to run – with Robertson and Hurst, good young attacking players, behind them. At least there would be less kicking than when Going was in control behind the scrum, while Hales and Batty on the wings knew the shortest way to the line, and Karam was piling up the points as a place kicker.

A most promising young referee from Wales was in charge of the match, Corris Thomas from Cardiff, having his first taste of big rugby, but before the match he was unworried, even though events on the field at Rodney Parade had drawn the best out of an experienced campaigner like Larry Lamb. The most interesting personality on the field was the half Irishman, John Duggan, on the wing from Leicester. He had scored some good ties and was eager for action.

Twenty-fourth Match

Versus East Midlands at Leicester, January 13.

New Zealand won by four goals, one penalty goal, four tries (43) to one goal and two penalty goals (12).

Weather: Fine. *Ground:* Good. *Crowd:* 9,000.

TEAMS:

EAST MIDLANDS: D. F. Whibley (*Leicester*); M. J. Duggan (*Leicester*), M. Yandle (*Leicester*), G. Phillips (*Northampton*), R. Morris (*Northampton*); B. Jones (*Leicester*), J. A. Allen (*Leicester*); D. L. Powell (*Northampton*, capt.), P. J. Wheeler (*Leicester*), P. Duffy (*Northampton*), P. J. Larter (*Northampton*), R. M. Wilkinson (*Cambridge University*), C. J. Baynes (*Leicester*), G. J. Adey (*Leicester*), I. Clayton (*Notts*). A. Davies sub. for B. Jones.

NEW ZEALAND: J. F. Karam; D. A. Hales, B. J. Robertson, I. A. Hurst, G. B. Batty; R. E. Burgess, G. L. Colling; G. J. Whiting, R. W. Norton, L. A. Clark, A. M. Haden, H. H. Macdonald, K. W. Stewart, A. R. Sutherland, I. A. Kirkpatrick (capt.).

Referee: Corris Thomas (Wales).

The match provided an overwhelming and thoroughly deserved victory for the All Blacks to the tune of 43 points to 12; they actually ran in for eight tries. It was by far their most delightful and attractive performance since the first match at Gloucester. Colling, Burgess, Hurst and Robertson, enjoying ready possession, played like the 1935 All Blacks and the 1945 Kiwis, as they ran with the ball. The crowd, disturbed at first by a couple of 'silly' incidents, gradually warmed to generous applause of the tourists as they ran the Midlands defence ragged.

Almost to a man, the critics praised the All Blacks and asked why such an approach had not been attempted before. It did not go unnoticed that neither Going nor Wyllie were on the field, as the New Zealand press always called them the 'field captains' . . . the cautious, dour men. In this match Kirkpatrick was not disturbed by their desire to keep it tighter, and the whole side ran attractively.

Their 43 points was not to be bettered again on tour (although equalled at Neath), and they must have been pleased at their reception. Joe Karam by kicking five goals, collected 11 points to reach his century for the tour, and such success could not have been enjoyed by a more engaging young player in his position. He moved into the select group of New Zealand kicking experts who have scored 100 points or more overseas.

Unfortunately, the East Midlands disappointed their supporters, for their much-vaunted pack with its powerful front five, faded away, and was outplayed before the end. Andy Haden outjumped Bob Wilkinson to reverse the form of the match against Cambridge University, and it was a mistake to continue to play the undergraduate at No. 5 and leave Larter near the front of the line. John Allen at scrum-half played bravely to use what little good possession he received and deserved his try, but young Bleddyn Jones (at outside-half) was injured and left the field at the interval to be replaced by Alan Davies, who found himself a little out of his depth.

The score was 18-6 at the interval, and then the All Blacks scored another 25 against six in the second half. For the touring party it was the return of Burgess to form, set free from his kicking chore, that impressed most and one felt that he was certain to go back into the test side against Ireland, as indeed he did. The try scorers for the All Blacks were Stewart, Burgess, Kirkpatrick, Robertson, Colling, Sutherland, Hurst, and Batty. Karam converted four and kicked a penalty. For the Midlands, Allen got a try and full-back Whibley converted it as well as kicking two penalties. For once the referee, and a Welshman too, brought no reported criticism from the All Blacks camp!

From Leicester the All Blacks moved into Ireland for the second time, to face a hard week with two stern matches at Cork and Dublin. The first was against Munster – whose reputation for vigorous and enthusiastic play was well known to the tourists – and the second, the vital last test against Ireland, upon which the hopes of British rugby depended. Incidentally, I had said at the first press conference (in London) at the start of the tour, that I thought Ireland would give the All Blacks the hardest match of the four countries and possibly defeat the tourists. I wasn't just guessing for I believed this test would be the last fling in search of success by such fine senior Irish players as McLoughlin, McBride, Kiernan, Gibson, and Kennedy.

Yet it was Munster who really frightened the life out of the tourists, for they were inspired by their devoted coach, no less a person than himself, the 'living saint' of Cork and a mighty fiery Lion, Noel Murphy. No one enters the hospitable City of Cork without giving the pass word, 'I know Tom Kiernan and Noel Murphy,' but, once said, then all is well for a 'hell of a game on the field' and a mighty 'massive' afterwards. Great rugby characters abound in the city and in the province of Munster and, like the Welsh, they appear to be inspired by the coming of a touring team!

Twenty-fifth Match
Versus Munster at Cork, January 16.
Drawn. One penalty goal (3) each.
Weather: Fine. *Ground:* Firm. *Crowd:* 15,000.
TEAMS:
MUNSTER: T. J. Kiernan (*Cork Constitution,* capt.); P. Parfrey (*U.C., Cork*), F. P. K. Bresnihan (*London Irish*), S. Dennison (*Garryowen*), J. Barry (*Dolphin*); B. J. McGann (*Cork Constitution*), D. Canniffe (*Cork Constitution*); P. O'Callaghan (*Dolphin*), J. Leahy (*Cork Constitution*), K. Keyes (*Sundays Well*), M. Keane (*U.C., Cork*), J. Madigan (*Bohemians*), J. Buckley (*Sundays Well*), T. Moore (*Highfield*), S. Deering (*Garryowen*).
NEW ZEALAND: T. J. Morris; B. G. Williams, D. A. Hales, R. M. Parkinson, G. R. Skudder; I. N. Stevens, G. L. Colling; S. McNicol, R. A. Urlich, K. K. Lambert, A. M. Haden, I. A. Eliason, A. J. Wyllie (capt.), A. R. Sutherland, B. Holmes.
Referee: D. W. Jones (England).

Ian Kirkpatrick, the non-stop playing captain, took a much deserved rest and Sidney Milton Going was to have led the tourists in his absence but he withdrew on the morning of the match with a thigh injury. Lyn Colling substituted for him, with Alex Wyllie assuming the role of captain. He had six current test players with him but whether the tourists underestimated the mighty men of Munster or wished to rest the majority of their test players, they accepted a known risk.

As it was, they only saved the game in injury time by kicking a penalty goal to match that scored by Munster, ten minutes after the interval. The mighty McGann, as the Irish call him, kicked the one for Munster and Trevor Morris equalised, with his most important kick of the tour, when all appeared lost for the tourists.

So the brave and vigorous effort by Munster to win their first match against the All Blacks, and become the first Irish side to do so, was thwarted but, only just, although the fiercely partisan crowd, in the end, was satisfied. They had rattled the tourists who often panicked, by stern forward play and tremendous tackling. They put the pressure on with high kicks, fast following up, and storming work at the rucks and mauls. Morris at full-back was erratic, Lyn Colling was under pressure as the Munster men drove through the line-out, and Ian Stevens was not by any means as happy trying to run the play at outside-half from Colling's service as he was when just supporting Going.

It was the first match in which the All Blacks had failed to score a try since the game against Llanelli and, at the start, there were a few outbreaks of rugby rioting before Referee Jones of England brought both sides to order. Yet it was the mighty McGann who was the Irish hero this day, punting superbly and putting the carrot up in front of his fiery forwards.

New Zealand, with three number eights in their back row, were at a disadvantage and, as Bob Howitt commented, there were too many forwards going backwards in defence and not enough forward in attack! The Munster flankers, Jim Buckley and Shaun Deering, were predatory in search of man and ball, while the line-out experts John Madigan and Moss Keane held the advantage at the line-out over Haden and Eliason.

Ernie Todd pulled no punches when, at the end of the match and greatly relieved by the last minute penalty from Morris, he said, 'This was our worst display of the tour. We have never handled, passed or kicked so badly. Still, as the game was near its end we were prepared to settle for a draw!' He was right and it could not have improved the confidence of the side for the even sterner test expected against the might of all Ireland on the Saturday.

McGann kicked his penalty from 40 yards after ten minutes of the second half to give Munster the lead and it looked as if they would win when injury time arrived. Then the twentieth penalty against Munster was given in the first minute of injury time and, from 30 yards, Morris, whose kicking had been erratic throughout the tour, landed the goal. When the final whistle went the All Blacks were glad to leave the field and during the evening the test XV for Dublin was announced.

It contained two changes, both behind the scrum and clearly inspired by the side's display at Leicester. Burgess replaced Stevens at outside-half and Ian Hurst won his first cap at second five-eighth or inside-centre to replace Mike Parkinson who, like Stevens, disappointed in the hurly-burly and crash tackling atmosphere of Cork. Ian Archibald Hurst, the 21-year-old agricultural student from Canterbury was almost an unknown until he appeared in an early All Black trial just before the tour, and earned his trip by marking Robertson closely. He had appeared in the fourth and fifth matches of the tour but was injured while playing well against the London Counties, and missed the next six matches, only to return and play in ten of the remaining 15, including the final match against the Barbarians. He should serve his country well in the future, when he has had more experience.

Ireland chose a powerful side with only one new cap in lock Kevin Michael Andrew Mays, the 23-year-old U.C. student who stood 6 ft. 5½ in. and weighed 16 st., to suggest that he was a worthy young partner for the 'master', Willie John McBride, making his 49th appearance for the old country. McBride always had the amusing saying going on tour, 'I hate small men!" as he, himself, was a tower of a man at 6 ft. 3 in. and 16 st., and thus the hard core of the Irish scrummage was assured.

The front row trio of McLoughlin, Kennedy and Lynch were Lions, holding 67 caps between them and every bit as hard and clever as any. They understood, completely, the New Zealand approach, while the back row included two big men in basketball expert Terence Moore at No. 8 and the rapidly improving Fergus Slattery, who was to play the game of his life for the Barbarians at Cardiff against the tourists. Only John Davidson from Dungannon, at 5 ft. 9½ in. and 13 st. 11 lb., failed to match the size of his opponents.

Behind, there was the elusive John Maloney at scrum-half and the strong reliable Barry John McGann at outside-half, in the 'Mick, Mick' English tradition, gaining his 17th cap. At threequarter Michael Gibson, a true hero of the 1971 Lions, was making his 39th appearance at the age of 29 but still not really happy about his back injury, suffered on the bone hard ground at Grange Road, during the Cambridge Centenary match. Alongside him was the equally experienced Kevin Flynn in his 34th year and, on the right-wing, Thomas Oliver Grace, who was to become the latest 'rugby saint' in Ireland, with Arthur McMaster on the left-wing. Behind them was the 'daddy' of them all, the most loved of Irish players, the most capped of British players, Thomas Joseph Kiernan, in his 35th year and playing in his 52nd match!

A remarkable band of brothers, from the North and South, bound together by a love of rugby and a respect for each other. Hard men, clever men with spirit and enthusiasm. Surely, they could save the reputation of British rugby?

Twenty-sixth Match

Versus Ireland at Lansdowne Road, Dublin, January 20.

Drawn. Ireland, two penalty goals, one try (10); New Zealand, one goal, one try (10).

Weather: Windy. *Ground:* Wet. *Crowd:* 52,000.

TEAMS:

IRELAND; T. J. Kiernan (*Cork Constitution,* capt.); T. O. Grace (*St Mary's*), M. K. Flynn (*Wanderers*), M. C. H. Gibson (*N.I.F.C.*), A. W. McMaster (*Ballymena*); B. G. McGann (*Cork Constitution*), J. J. Moloney (*St Mary's*); R. J. McLoughlin (*Blackrock Coll.*), K. W. Kennedy (*London Irish*), J. F. Lynch (*St Mary's*), W. J. McBride (*Ballymena*), K. Mays (*U.C., Dublin*), J. F. Slattery (*Blackrock Coll.*), T. Moore (*Highfield*), J. Davidson (*Dungannon*).

NEW ZEALAND: J. F. Karam; B. G. Williams, B. J. Robertson, I. A. Hurst, G. B. Batty; R. E. Burgess, S. M. Going; K. K. Lambert, R. W. Norton, G. J. Whiting, P. J. Whiting, H. H. Macdonald, A. J. Wyllie, A. R. Sutherland, I. A. Kirkpatrick (capt.).

Referee: M. Joseph (Wales).

It proved to be a match of three separate periods. A match the All Blacks almost lost after being clearly in sight of victory, but one they did not deserve to lose and should have won, yet they reckoned without the fighting spirit of the Irish. It is rare that the likeable Irish men enjoy good fortune in their rugby but on this day, the 'little people' were with them, seeing that they came to no great harm!

During the first ten minutes Ireland were on top, scrummaging superbly but then the All Blacks gained control, and remained in charge for almost an hour, only to allow the fighting Irish to recover and take control in the final ten minutes. In that vital period, Ireland, trailing at 3-10, fought back to 10–10 and shared a draw. Had the mighty McGann's conversion attempt gone between the posts, instead of sailing just wide of the near upright, then Ireland would have won, and the of the near upright, then Ireland would have won, and the All Blacks suffered defeat for the first time in the land of the 'little people'. Such a thought still sends shivers down the broad backs of the All Blacks.

However, the All Blacks failed to achieve the 'Grand Slam' with four victories over the Home Countries, but they survived without defeat and that was more than the folks at home expected when they called them the 'worst side ever to leave New Zealand'. The 1924–25 side, a much stronger combination, achieved only three victories as they did not meet Scotland owing to a dispute (or rather a 'hang over' from the 1905 tour). The 'Invincibles' were unbeaten on their tour to set a tremendous target for succeeding sides, but one cannot say with any certainty that they would have beaten the magnificent Scottish XV of that year – a team that won all its four matches in the Five Nations Championship.

It was a considerable achievement by the 1972/3 All Blacks, yet they failed in their major objective because of the caution that had dominated their play throughout, and their lack of flair, for when 10–3 in the lead they should have cracked on regardless but, instead, they faltered and were caught from behind!

Even the N.Z. press party dared to criticise and N.Z.P.A.'s John Brooks sent out a strong piece about the extreme caution and heedless kicking when strong running would have benefited. Terry McLean's piece in *The Times* was cleverly headed, 'When you play a big fish never let him off the hook'. McLean argued that the All Blacks had Ireland safely 'hooked' and then allowed the line go loose when, in the eight most hectic minutes of the tour, Ireland recovered. Perhaps it was at this stage that the All Blacks ran out of luck – the luck that had saved them against Wales at Cardiff!

At 10–3, Going was penalised once again, despite N.Z. protests that he never put the ball in the scrum at an angle, and the mighty McGann landed a 28 yard goal to make it 10–6. Now Ireland were within striking range as the All Blacks had slackened off and could not regain their grip. It was the veteran full-back, gallant Tom Kiernan, who had set the recovery in motion before McGann's second penalty goal, by charging away from his own '25' and getting to near the half way line to set up an attack. Soon after, Going was penalised for the fourth time for 'not straight', and McGann with his goal revived the smouldering fires of the Irish.

There was just a chance, but no more than a chance, that they would score again. The forwards and especially, Moore, McBride and McLoughlin, put everything they had into it. From a scrum near to the N.Z. ten yard line, Moloney broke bravely on the blind side. He drew the lively but anxious Batty into him, as Going was not then near the scene of action, and the pass was carefully pouched by the 6 ft. 2 in. long-striding Tom Grace. There was roughly 40 yards to go with only Karam ahead of Grace, and rather than risk the tackle or the time needed for evading action, the wing kicked over Karam's head and the ball rolled on over the goal line. The chase was on . . . with Grace a nose in front of Burgess seeking to get to the ball first and save the match. Grace maintained his lead and then with as glorious a dive as was ever launched at Lansdowne Road, the Irishman got the touch and a try, just as the ball neared the dead ball line!

The crowd erupted and many raced on to the field. Ireland were level and this was quiete incredible, for never had a side looked more beaten than them. Imagine how the poor All Blacks must have felt, as they took guard on their goal line, and the mighty McGann prepared for his conversion attempt. This kick, if successful, would boot Ireland into rugby history and there was nothing less than the 'presidency' for McGann if he could do it. The silence was eerie and tense, as the rather rotund, effervescing outside-half moved into kick. Bang . . . the ball rose and sailed to the posts. It looked a good one, but then alas, at the last second, the ball veered away, a matter of inches, and sailed outside the post!

Ireland had just failed in their memorable challenge and the All Blacks were safe. The wind, as much as anything else, had saved them although it would have been extremely hard on them had they lost this match. Yet in the long run, after all the arguments, they would have had to blame themselves, for not showing greater courage and going for more points. The policy of safety first nearly destroyed them.

After eight minutes Ireland, following their good start, were three points in the lead. Playing with the wind they drove the All Blacks back and, from 47 yards out on the left, the tourists conceded a penalty at a scrum, and the mighty McGann kicked a goal. Cheers greeted his effort but he has never been Ireland's first choice as place-kicker since Kiernan has been the master craftsman over the years. In all McGann had six attempts and succeeded with two; a couple more good ones and Ireland would have achieved their greatest victory.

Slowly the All Blacks assumed command with some fine forward play that dampened down the heat of the Irish effort. Referee Meirion Joseph kept a close eye on proceedings and allowed neither side to get away with anything in the struggle for supremacy.

After 28 minutes the All Blacks achieved the lead. Ireland won a scrum 20 yards out and Maloney attempted a break but he was cleverly robbed by Going, now playing at his best, who gathered and then twisted and turned to bore his way through the defensive Irish wall, and gain the open ground for a final dash over the goal line, without a green sleeve touching his crouching form. It was a vital try; a typical Going effort; a repeat of many similar dashes produced during the tour. Joe Karam landed a superb conversion and the three points lead gave the tourists the inspiration they needed.

They could smell the Grand Slam and see the champagne ahead of them. This could be New Zealand's finest hour. It was 6–3 at half time with the use of the wind to come. They were almost home and dry! McGann failed with penalty attempts after the interval and then in the 18th minute of the second half, the All Blacks scored another try which at the time appeared to settle the fate of the Irish. Lambert won the ball at a ruck and fed Burgess who ran a dozen yards and sent in-field to Wyllie in full cry.

He set the goal line as his target, even though Kiernan barred the way, and Wyllie got there, through Kiernan! A typical N.Z. forward effort and as valuable a try as Wyllie ever scored, but Karam could not convert. At the time, this did not appear to New Zealand supporters, as a serious miss, but later it was the margin between victory and a drawn match.

Now it was that New Zealand relaxed, believing they were safe and, rather than risk possible errors, kicked away possession, and not particularly accurately. A few of Burgess's kicks were poor and the side eased off, even at forward, and the Irish pack, against the collar for some time, sensed the easing as McBride told me later, and stirred themselves for a special effort. No one could judge better than McBride, who has played so many matches against New Zealand opposition at home and down under.

There followed the great Irish recovery and a drawn match. Terry McLean in his *Times* report could not resist a crack at the Welsh, the nation he loves so deeply, by saying, 'It was a proud moment for Ireland. And, come to think of it, it was not a bad sort of day for the New Zealanders either. After all, what happened to the Welsh last time they played at Lansdowne Road?' The All Blacks and their camp followers just could not knock that Welsh 'chip' from their shoulders – or was it an inferiority complex about the ebullient Welsh, developed as a result of the efforts of Barry John, Carwyn James, John Dawes and other Welsh Lions?

Carwyn James had this to say in *The Observer* after the match: 'It was difficult to understand the All Blacks attitude and approach, once they were at 10–3, bearing in mind there was so much at stake. Despite mounting criticism of their play during the tour, they were on the verge of winning all four home internationals, an achievement which did not fall to any of their illustrious predecessors. They seemed in full command and have only themselves to blame for not making history . . . The Irish are nothing if not unpredictable!'

So Tom Kiernan left the field a happy man. His team had stopped the All Blacks from achieving the Grand Slam . . . a great performance . . . but how much was their recovery helped

The Barbarian team that defeated New Zealand at Cardiff Arms Park by 23–11. Standing (*left to right*): E. M. Lewis (touch judge), G. W. Lewis (hon. sec.), J. V. Pullin, W. J. McBride, R. Wilkinson, D. L. Quinnell, A. B. Carmichael, D. Duckham, G. Domercq (referee), D. O. Spyer (touch judge); sitting: G. O. Edwards, C. M. H. Gibson, Brig. H. L. G. Hughes (President), S. J. Dawes (capt.), H. Waddell (vice President), J. C. Bevan, R. McLoughlin; in front: J. F. Slattery, T. David, P. Bennett, J. P. R. Williams

Slattery scores the Barbarians' second try

John Williams, the Barbarians' full back, going flat out for the line as Batty desperately tries to tackle. There was no stopping Williams and he scored the third fine Barbarians' try. *Below:* John Dawes, the Barbarians' captain, being carried from the field in triumph after a magnificent game in which both teams played exciting rugby

by the All Blacks? Even Ernie Todd, Bob Duff, Terry McLean and Uncle Tom Cobley and all could not answer that one . . . only the 'little people' wearing those special emerald green jerseys, and unseen to all but Tom Kiernan, as they raced over Lansdowne Road's green, green grass!

13 *The Lions Return*

The All Blacks returned to Wales on the Monday after the Irish Test, flying in to Glamorgan Airport from Dublin with mixed feelings, for their last matches in the Principality, where Ian Kirkpatrick had told reporters after the Irish Test, his side had met the strongest opposition. Wales, he felt, did best against them in the tests. Their penultimate match, and the last against all Welsh opposition, was on the Wednesday at the Gnoll Ground, Neath, and they indicated they had no intention of conceding it, despite the nature of the Barbarians match on the Saturday at Cardiff.

Sid Going hobbled into Porthcawl, and there were three different opinions as to his ankle injury. The first was that he could not possibly play on the Saturday; the second was that he would soon be fit and help defeat the Barbarians, while the third was that he was throwing a 'Hollywood', a New Zealand phrase for any player – but especially opponents of the home crowd – feigning injury. Whatever criticism one may make of Going, I do not think he was a 'Hollywood' man. I once recall an incident in 1971, when it was suggested that John Dawes was throwing a 'Hollywood', and I hated it. As events were to prove, Going was injured and in pain, and the suggestion of 'Hollywood' should be treated with the contempt it deserves.

Lindsay Colling deputised for Going at Neath, partnering Bob Burgess to suggest that the All Blacks would run the ball at Neath and 'give it a go'. Alan Sutherland had an eye infection and Ron Urlich a bruised knee, so they were not considered, but ten players who had appeared in one or more of the four tests were on duty and this spelled trouble (in a 'big way' as was proved) for the combined Aberavon/Neath side despite the brave utterances of their coach, Grahame Hodgson.

One did not expect them to win because the history of the efforts of the two clubs in harness was not a happy one. They were great rivals and, like 'oil and water', never mixed or blended; each club on its own would have done better. Eight Neath and Seven Aberavon players formed the side, with three Welsh and one Scottish international in the pack, but John Bevan of Aberavon withdrew with an injury on the morning of the match and was substituted by a Neath player, the smallest first class player in Wales, if not the world, in representative football, David Parker, at 5 ft. 4 in. and 9 st. 'dripping wet'.

Yet there was considerable enthusiasm for the match and tickets were at a premium. The town was full of enthusiasts long before the kick off, and the hotels and grill bars did a roaring trade. Neath were at the top of the Welsh Club championship table at the time, and holders of the W.R.U. K.O. Cup, but their biggest forward, Brian Thomas, who had toured New Zealand with Wales in 1969, was not selected as he was unfit following an injury.

Everything depended, for the Combined side, upon the play of their forwards but the big, strong and experienced pack fielded by the tourists, with five test players in it, suggested that life would be hard for the Welshmen, but not quite as hard as it proved!

The All Blacks gave the Welshmen a real 'hiding' with running rugby while producing their best performance in Wales, and the match disproved the suggestion by Terry O'Connor in the *Daily Mail* that 'It could be war again'. The All Blacks raced over for their tries and the Gnoll crowd cheered. Even if one spectator had a verbal swearing match with Grant Batty, this did not diminish the pace and quality of the All Blacks football, as successfully they came in out of the cold in Wales.

As Bob Howitt, commented in the *Western Mail*, the 'Wellington boot was on the Gnoll foot after this trouncing,' referring to the heavy defeat by the Lions of Wellington province in 1971 (47–9), as the Combined Welsh side went down 43–3. The All Blacks scored seven tries, converting six of them as well as kicking a penalty goal and the Combined side got one penalty. The tally of 43 points equalled that achieved at Leicester, as the highest of the tour, but the winning margin was 40 points, the highest ever achieved by a N.Z. side in Wales, and thoroughly deserved.

On the Saturday, the Barbarians were to score 23 against them, which was the highest tally of the tour, and the highest total ever achieved by a team in the British Isles against a full All Blacks side. The New Zealand side against Neath got into the mood and played as they should have done throughout the tour, and it was said at the Afon Lido after the match that I would not give them the praise they deserved. The *Western Mail* on Thursday morning said: 'All Blacks run to superb victory,' and the opening paragraph read: 'With a devastating display of skill and power the All Blacks proved themselves in Wales at the Gnoll yesterday'... 'I can only congratulate the tourists on their fine display which must help to wipe out some of the unhappy memories of previous matches and reveal to Welshmen that the tourists are capable of such good play.'

If they had played like this more often, and especially in Wales, how much more pleasant the tour would have been, and Welshmen would have accepted them more readily. Welshmen never turn their backs on good rugby, as they proved in this match and again on the Saturday. They love good football and while the Combined team's supporters were disappointed, they were sportsmen enough and lovers of the game, to applaud the tourists.

The N.Z. forwards went superbly and after 15 minutes took charge, supplying their backs with regular good possession; setting up rucks, winning them, switching direction and really rampaging. The backs, with Colling and Burgess in perfect unison at half-back, ran delightfully and the wings were often in possession. The Combined back division's defence was cut to shreds and the tackling became weaker and weaker while the cover was non existent.

The Combined side disappointed themselves as well as their supporters and, as full-back Joe Karam kicked seven goals and scored a try to collect 19 points, he equalled Trevor Morris's record for the tour, of the same number against the Combined Services at Twickenham. Little Joe was at the top – the real discovery of the tour.

Twenty-seventh match
Versus Neath-Aberavon at Neath, January 24.
New Zealand won by six goals, one penalty goal and one try (43) to one penalty goal (3).
Weather: Dull. *Ground:* Soft. *Crowd:* 14,800
TEAMS:
NEATH-ABERAVON: W. Davies (*Neath*); D. Jenkins (*Neath*), G. Ball (*Neath*) capt., J. Thomas (*Aberavon*), K. Collier (*Neath*); D. Parker (*Neath*), C. Shell (*Aberavon*); G. Shaw (*Neath*), M. Howells (*Aberavon*), R. Lewis (*Neath*), W. T. Mainwaring (*Aberavon*), A. J. Martin (*Aberavon*), W. D. Morris (*Neath*), W. Lauder (*Neath*), O. Alexander (*Aberavon*).
NEW ZEALAND: J. F. Karam; D. A. Hales, I. A. Hurst, M. Sayers, G. B. Batty; R. E. Burgess, G. L. Colling; G. J. Whiting, R. W. Norton, S. McNicol, H. H. Macdonald, A. M. Haden, K. W. Stewart, A. J. Wyllie, I. A. Kirkpatrick (capt.). *Replacement:* B. G. Williams for Batty.
Referee: P. E. Hughes (England).

After 14 minutes it was 3–3, with Karam kicking the first penalty goal of the match and Alan Martin, the tall lock, replying with one for the Combined side. By half time it was 15–3 and the signs were ominous. At the end it was 43–3, and the All Blacks try scorers were Kirkpatrick and Karam in the first half, with both converted by Karam. In the second half, Batty, Hurst, Burgess, then Burgess again and Sayers, with Karam missing only one conversion. This win delighted every member of the touring party and Manager Todd commented, 'I am delighted, for the boys produced some really good football – the stuff that Welshmen appreciate.' Alas, it should have come much sooner!

Later in the evening, the All Blacks selected their team for the final match and liaison officer, Handel Rogers, rang me from the Afon Lido. Sid Going was in the side and the three running midfield backs, Burgess, Hurst and Robertson, while Scown played on the flank because Sutherland was unfit, and he was a quicker player about the field, while another good loose forward, hooker Urlich, replaced Norton, who was surprised at being dropped. It looked a good side, and inspired by the victories at Neath and Leicester, must have felt confident it could hold its own with the Barbarians, in a running match.

When the Barbarians side was announced in the previous week, hon. secretary Geoffrey Windsor Lewis, a modest likeable fellow, much respected in the game, said, 'The Barbarians have chosen a good side; the best in the circumstances, and it is determined to win, but by playing good running rugby.' This was the challenge and, in selecting the side they did, the All Blacks accepted it.

In the original Barbarians side, Gerald Davies, Mervyn Davies, and Barry Llewelyn were included, and it would therefore have contained 12 Lions. However, the two Davies fell out on the Saturday morning before the match, and Llewelyn withdrew earlier with a knee cartilage injury. John Bevan came in on the wing; another non-capped player, Tom David of Llanelli, moved into the back row, and Sandy Carmichael replaced Llewelyn as prop.

So this strong side still had 12 Lions, six in front and six behind, with David and the young Cambridge undergraduate, Bob Wilkinson, as the only two non-capped players. They were new Barbarians, as all the other 13 were members of the Club, most of them from before the 1971 Lions tour. Thus the Barbarians had stuck to their club traditions: had picked members and included non-capped players, and NOT a Lions side, although earlier the All Blacks had complained that they had been conned into an extra 'test'. It has been the same on the nine previous tours, since the fixture was launched in 1948 to raise funds to send the Wallabies home via the U.S.A. and Canada!

It was suggested to the Barbarians that they should meet on the Tuesday and have four days with Carwyn James as coach in true Lions style, but the President of the Club, a world figure in the game, Brig. H. L. Glyn Hughes, the first allied medical officer into Belsen at the end of World War II, politely argued that it must be a Barbarians affair and not escalated. It is true that several people were consulted about the composition of the team, and Carwyn James was one of them. In fact, the Club secretary, Geoffrey Lewis chatted with me about it as far back as early November and we both sensed then, BEFORE the Cardiff Club match with the tourists, that January 27 would be a big occasion!

In all sincerity, he wanted the best possible Barbarians side, and as long as he could get his committee and president to agree, he was more than willing to have one non-capped player in accordance with traditions. We all wanted John Dawes as captain. I had wanted him to lead Wales when Lewis was injured, and still believe the suggestion was valid and could have proved successful, especially after seeing 'Smiling Syd' lead the Barbarians!

After the captain, the next important thing was the hard core of the pack, and this had to come from Ireland with McBride and McLoughlin. Incidentally, when Ray McLoughlin arrived in Cardiff for the match, he had a huge brief case with him, stuffed full with business files and notes, and McBride immediately christened it, 'The Plan for Victory!'

The loose forwards would be Irish and Welsh, and the uncapped player was to be Bob Wilkinson, the undergraduate who had played so well for his Varsity against the All Blacks. The halves had to be Edwards and Bennett, with Williams at full-back and a Lions threequarter line – Davies, Dawes, Gibson and Duckham. A good side but, as Dawes told me, 'As long as we are not too rusty, we could do well!'

Twenty-eighth Match.
Versus the Barbarians at Cardiff Arms Park, January 27.
Barbarians won by two goals, one penalty and two tries (23) to one penalty and two tries (11)
Weather: Fine. *Ground:* Firm. *Crowd:* 50,800.
TEAMS:
BARBARIANS: J. P. R. Williams (*London Welsh*); D. Duckham (*Coventry*), S. J. Dawes (*London Welsh*) capt., C. M. H. Gibson (*N.I.F.C.*), J. C. Bevan (*Cardiff*); P. Bennett (*Llanelli*), G. O. Edwards (*Cardiff*); R. J. McLoughlin (*Backrock Coll.*), J. V. Pullin (*Bristol*), A. M. Carmichael (*West of Scot.*), W. J. McBride (*Ballymena*), R. M. Wilkinson (*Camb. Univ.*), T. David (*Llanelli*), D. L. Quinnell (*Llanelli*), J. F. Slattery (*Blackrock Coll.*).
NEW ZEALAND: J. F. Karam; B. G. Williams, B. J. Robertson, I. A. Hurst, G. B. Batty; R. E. Burgess, S. M. Going; G. J. Whiting, R. A. Urlich, K. K. Lambert, H. H. Macdonald, P. J. Whiting, A. I. Scown, A. J. Wyllie, I. A. Kirkpatrick (capt.).
G. L. Colling substituted for Going during last 20 mins.
Referee: Georges Domercq (French R. F.).

The crowd was put in the mood for a magnificent afternoon

both by the singing of the national anthems, and by the New Zealand *Haka* (Maori symbolic tribal war dance) performed for the one and only time on tour. It was a winner, and as Manager Todd had whispered to me at the pre-match lunch function given by the Welsh Brewers and the Welsh Rugby Writers Association, that I was in for a pleasant surprise before the kick off, I guessed what would happen. It was a P.R. chore that should have been carried out at every match. The players voted against this before the tour started and it was a vital blow against tradition!

Bennett started the match for the Barbarians, kicking towards the River Taff End, and the crowd had just settled following the preliminary skirmishing when, in the fourth minute, the Barbarians rocked the crowd and the stands with a magnificent try that gave the match the hall mark of quality. Perhaps, it was the greatest try ever scored in the first five minutes of a representative match – certainly, there has never been a better one!

Right wing Bryan Williams, was sent away in the loose and nearing the half way, he put in a good attacking high punt to the centre of the field, which rolled away into the Barbarians '25'. Bennett was back to chase it and, after fielding and turning round, he was faced with the oncoming N.Z. forwards on a broad front. At that moment, he decided against the traditional kick to touch, which any player in any big match would have done 999 times out of a possible 1000. Instead, he set off with a series of bewildering side steps which left the first four tourists flat footed and clutching at the air. Then he handed on to John Pullin, who also refused to kick to touch with English caution!

Instead, he galloped a few yards and handed on to the alert Tom David. He made ground and then fed Dawes inside him, and the Barbarians captain sliced through cleverly, as good a break as he has ever made. Soon he was in the N.Z. half of the field, with the alarm signals sounding among the tourists as they all haired back to the left corner flag which was the Barbarians target.

The crowd had jumped to its feet; they had sensed a special moment in rugby history. They were ready for a great try or a brilliant save. It was the 1971 Lions skill and counter attack all over again. Then Dawes, a fine reader of the game, saw his avenue closing and threw a high pass to his left, where Quinnell was pounding away at top speed for a 16 st. forward. He took the pass with his finger tips and, as he fell, threw a good pass towards the left touch line for John Bevan, also at full stretch.

This was just over 30 yards from the N.Z. line, but no one had noticed that Gareth Edwards was steaming through the field, like a thoroughbred, and when he took the pass intended for Bevan, he was really 'motoring', as Doug Smith used to say of his players in 1971. The cover defence was closing, so Edwards had to go, as quickly as ever his strong legs had carried him in the past. He could see the goal line and the corner flag; he could hear Grant Batty in full cry behind him. He was not going to be stopped and then, with a spectacular dive was over the line as Batty tackled him.

Up got Edwards with the ball and trotted back, while the whole crowd yelled and cheered in appreciation. What a movement; what a daring counter attack; what a chase; what a great try; what a moment to savour. Even the press box applauded, for this was one of the really great moments, and what a boost for the Barbarians! They had snatched the lead, so early on; they were a Lions team now, employing Lions' methods and the old firm of Smith and James were in business again, while Dawes knew then that there was no rust on his brilliant rugby machine, 1971 model!

The conversion attempt by Bennett failed but no one worried about this and all credit to the All Blacks for they set about the task of seeking tries themselves. It was good hard rugby; no exhibition stuff, and players were often winded, temporarily, in stern tackles. John Williams brought off some superb tackles in defence of his line and one on the flying Batty, was a beauty, and saved a certain try. Edwards and Bennett were comfortable in attack and defence and kicking well while Going appeared to be below his best in face of intelligent spoiling for, as planned, Quinnell, David and Edwards gave him no peace, and his service to the alert Burgess suffered.

Tom David was in tremendous form, 'taking the play to the enemy', which so few British flank forwards had been able to do through the tour. However, at the line-out and the rucks the tourists had the edge, and one sensed that Referee

Domercq in trying to be as unobtrusive as possible, did not whistle too frequently for line-out infringements. Peter Whiting got up high and won a lot of ball for his side. Batty was looking for work and made a couple of good runs and then after 33 minutes, Going was caught by Edwards and a maul followed from which Wyllie emerged without the ball, on the wrong side, and was penalised. Bennett from 26 yards kicked the goal and the Barbarians went further ahead.

In the next ten minutes, including injury time, before the interval they were to pile on the pressure. They forced a scrum ten yards out, half way between the posts and the left corner flag. New Zealand won the heel but Edwards caught Going again, and the alert Slattery was there to gather the ball and crash his way over as he was tackled by Karam and Williams. A good aggressive try, and Bennett kicked the goal to make it 13–0. Obviously, the All Blacks were being shaken out of their stride by the continuity of the Barbarians attack, and their pace and accuracy, supported by constant switching, that was so difficult to cover. They had complained that few sides had run at them, and this was what Secretary Lewis, had meant by good running rugby!

Then, in the first minute of injury time, the Barbarians got another try. Slattery caught Burgess, dealing with a poor pass from Going, brought him down and Quinnell was up quickly to gather, and hand on to Dawes who, with a beautifully timed pass across a defender, set Bevan charging away. The wing shook off Bryan Williams before turning inside a little to charge right through corner flaggers, Hurst and Karam, and crash over the line for a typical Bevan try that recalled memories of his 'through a brick wall' one for the Lions against Canterbury.

It was not converted but now the Barbarians were ahead by 17–0, the biggest total scored by a team against the tourist on the tour, and there was still the second half to come. Unless the All Blacks could stage a fantastic recovery, they were a beaten side, but then no All Blacks side ever gives up easily, and the Seventh 'Cavalry' decided to have a go themselves at the running game and the crowd loved it.

After five minutes of the second half, Karam kicked a penalty goal, after Kirkpatrick had lost the ball when tackled on the line dealing with a kick ahead that should have brought a try, and Karam had failed with his first penalty attempt. Three minutes later the All Blacks got their first try – and a good one. Bryan Williams came in from the blind side wing on the right and Karam joined the line to make the complete overlap for Batty who raced outside Duckham and scored in the left corner, but Karam could not convert although it looked much better for the All Blacks at 17–7.

Gibson hurt his hand and had to have it strapped and one sensed that his back, injured at Cambridge, was still giving him trouble. The All Blacks were going better although Going was fading, being caught several times for 'not straight' at a scrummage, and this time it was a French referee who did the judging! After 20 minutes of the second half, Going hobbled off, and ended his tour in the British Isles.

Lin Colling came on for him and his smooth passing had the All Blacks swinging along behind the scrum. Bennett kicked wide from 56 yards and then Batty and David had a 'brush' on the touch line before a cool David patted the 'small' man on the head. Obviously 'little Ginger' was steamed up at such treatment but the crowd booed and he gave them the 'fingers' sign. More booing . . !

Still, Batty could not be kept quiet. All Blacks passing was not too clever from the loose and so Hurst kicked through to the left with Duckham in field in defence. Batty gathered and chipped the ball cleverly past John Williams, to dash round, gather again, and cross the line for his 17th try of the tour.

The score was now 17–11 which meant that another goal would bring the All Blacks level after a mighty recovery. The crowd were enthralled by the fine play and the manner in which the two sides ran at each other, tackled and covered. This was high grade rugby . . . a better contest than any of the previous 25 matches. Obviously, the next side to score would probably win in the end.

Colling put in a clearing kick towards the right touch line, which Duckham fielded and set off in field with a series of swerves and side steps. Then Quinnell supported him and handed on to Dawes who again ran beautifully before handing on to John Williams. He was checked and Gibson took over with a 'duck under' a tackle and on to Slattery, dashing up strongly. Finally, there was John Williams again, to take Slattery's pass and cleverly avoid a high Batty tackle and crash over in the corner. Bennett kicked a superb goal off the touch line and it was 23–11 with ten minutes to go. The All Blacks needed 12 points to draw and 13 to win, but it was rather too much for them. Yet they tried, and tried hard. Once they had a 3–2 overlap but wasted the chance and the Barbarians stood firm, to leave the field with a very big prize indeed, as the teams were engulfed by the crowd.

Dawes and Kirkpatrick were hoisted aloft upon eager shoulders to receive the rare but warmly awarded Arms Park accolade. The crowd had enjoyed every minute of the match and wanted to show their appreciation. They sang 'Now is the hour' and the tour, that had rumbled its way through dull and dark days, had emerged into the sunlight before it was too late. The All Blacks had come into the warmth of the Arms Park out of the cold, and even they must have realised, at long last, what British rugby was all about, and what made the British Lions tick in 1971.

The brilliance of the Barbarians' backs and the combination with their loose forwards. The steady work in the tight; the superb tackling and covering in depth; all this fine play had the trade mark 'Lions' written all over it! John Dawes proved once again that he is quite the best captain produced by the British Isles in twenty years.

Yet the most enjoyable feature of the match was the fact that the people in Wales were able to see the 1971 Lions in action and realise, 'in the flesh', why they won the series in New Zealand, and also watch the All Blacks enjoying themselves while playing a running game to win back many friends. A great pity it had not happened sooner. Terry O'Connor had written in the Auckland *Eight O'Clock*, early in the tour, that the 1971 Lions played 10 man rugby in the tests and he accepted the All Blacks accusations of this as he was a 'realist'. I can recall the Lions running with the ball in the Second and Third tests and scoring fine tries. Indeed, I remembered those two fine tests, at Christchurch and Wellington, while watching this match!

All Blacks manager, Ernie Todd came to the press box to talk on the radio but, before he did, he told me how much he had enjoyed the match. Bob Duff told me before the dinner that it was enjoyable but not 'test rugby'. More's the pity! All test rugby should be as this match, with the sides running at each other. What thrills; what rugby splendour, and how much both sides enjoyed it.

The All Blacks went back to their dressing room. Some of them sat with their heads bowed and held in their hands, as much due to fatigue as disappointment. Ian Kirkpatrick, much impressed by the day, sent for a couple of bottles of whisky and asked each player to toast, with him, one of the greatest matches, and the one and only 'John Dawes'. A fine action, and one that was a fitting end to the tour.

John Dawes said, 'It was a great challenge for us, as we were expected to play like the 1971 Lions. It was not just good Barbarians rugby, but British rugby at its best.'

Ernie Todd commented, 'The Barbarians played a type of rugby we have not met on tour before.' Later at the dinner he said, 'We have always wanted to see this rugby on tour. There was a fantastic atmosphere at the Cardiff Arms Park, but we think the Barbarians 'pulled the wool over our eyes' and got away with the Golden Fleece but left us with the crutchings! Yet we salute the Barbarians for their champagne rugby. I am sure our players learned a lot today. We will always remember this match.'

Brig. Glyn Hughes told the teams and guests: 'It is the best match ever in the series against touring teams and we are delighted to be back in Cardiff, after being away for two matches (1967 and 1970). We are not a Lions team, but a scratch side, although the influence of the 1971 Lions was very strong. We are indebted to the management of Doug Smith and Carwyn James on that tour. I believe the victory and the manner of it will provide a big boost to morale in British rugby.'

Ian Kirkpatrick was made an honorary Barbarian at the end of the dinner and he was delighted. Now he was a blood brother, and honoured as had been every N.Z. captain since Jack Manchester in 1936. His final cloud had passed away and the sun was shining for him and his team. It was really there all the time, but had been ignored by a team that had been unnecessarily suspicious, especially of the Welsh!

14 *Finale in France*

When Ian Kirkpatrick arrived in London in October, he said he expected the four matches in France to be the hardest of the tour – in some respects he was right. The tour ended at the magnificent new Parc des Princes Stadium at approximately 4.30 p.m. (French time) on February 10. The leg-weary All Blacks left the field a completely beaten side and the French looked, on the day, the best side in Europe. The All Blacks looked no better, probably worse, than they had been at Llanelli at the start of the tour. Some of this was as a result of tour weariness but mostly it was due to the fact that, tactically, they had not developed. On that day in Paris, one hoped the New Zealand nine and ten man rugby was buried for ever.

Their first stop in France was at Tarbes where they met a selected Regional XV, and the game provided them with a good taste of French rugby to make good Kirkpatrick's claim that nothing would be easy there on the field of play, but that the enthusiasm and hospitality off the field would be more than enough. The Selected XV contained many seasoned and experienced players with a good knowledge of New Zealand rugby. One forward, no less than Benoit Dauga himself, must indeed have known as much about it as some of the younger New Zealand players themselves!

With him were Andre Campaes on the wing, who was recalled to the national XV in the following week, the tall Jean Pierre Bastiat at lock with line-out expert Alan Plantefol, prop Jean Louis Azarete and flanker Jean Claude Skrela, plus full-back Jean-Michel Aguirre. These players provided really good opposition and Tarbes turned out in strength and good whistling voice to greet the tourists.

Twenty-ninth Match
Versus a Selected French XV at Tarbes, January 31.
New Zealand won by one goal and two penalties (12) to a penalty (3)
Scorers: For Selected XV: Aguirre one penalty (second half). For New Zealand: Morris and Williams penalties (first half). Robertson try and Williams con. (second half).
Weather: Damp. *Ground:* Soft. *Crowd:* 17,000.
TEAMS:
FRENCH SELECTION: J. M. Aguirre; M. Lacoste, J. Pecune, P. Nadal, A. Campaes; A. Morrettie, G. Pardies; J. L. Azarete, J. L. Ugartemendia, A. Darrieusecq, A. Plantefol, J. P. Bastiat, P. Peron, B. Dauga (capt.), J. C. Skrela.
NEW ZEALAND: T. J. Morris; B. G. Williams, B. J. Robertson, R. M. Parkinson, G. R. Skudder; I. N. Stevens, G. L. Colling; A. McNicol, R. A. Urlich, L. Clark, P. J. Whiting, I. M. Eliason, B. Holmes, A. R. Sutherland, and I. A. Kirkpatrick (capt.).

The Frenchmen gave the All Blacks a stern game but the tourists deserved their win. As Bob Howitt said, 'The French showed a reluctance to commit defenders to the tackle before passing, and made several handling errors with the greasy ball, but they outscrummaged the All Blacks and their forwards were determined in the loose.'

The All Blacks were impressed with full-back Aguirre, who was to be selected for France, but had to withdraw because of injury, being replaced by Cantoni, who was then injured during the match. In this game, Aguirre looked an impressive place kicker although he landed only one goal. Peter Whiting had a good match for the tourists while Robertson got their try following a dummy scissors and a good burst.

From Tarbes the tourists moved on to the city of Lyons, to meet a French Under-23 team at the Stade Gerland. The French side included eight full internationals after the five at Tarbes and this brought forth the comment from Terry McLean that the French were using the matches as trials to find the best XV to oppose New Zealand in the test in Paris. Quite true, the French never miss a trick, but selecting a French XV, and the best at that, is quite the hardest task in modern rugby. Every region has its own heroes and it is never easy to satisfy everyone or get the best fifteen players to perform in unison. If the French could blend their best XV every season, and then get the side to play at its best, they would be continuous world champions. Of this there NO doubt!

The All Blacks did not play well in the first half but improved and were the better side in the second half, to deserve their win which in figures, at least, appeared comfortable. The All Blacks were hard pressed at times but Stevens, formally a scrum-half, and playing in the position for the first time on tour as Going was unfit and Colling was resting, did extremely well.

The match was turned before the interval when the All Blacks were leading 3–0, as Grant Batty raced away for a try which gave the tourists the confidence they needed. Previously they were in trouble, defensively trying to hold out and contain the clever running and sleight of hand of midfield attackers, Pebeyre, Berot, Maso and Bertranne.

Batty finished the day in great style and was given his best reception of the tour, for his clever running and try getting. He could have been a match winner throughout the tour and should have received a great deal more of the ball as he knew his way to the line. A tough aggressive little fellow, on and off the field.

Thirtieth Match
Versus French Under-23 XV at Stade Gerland, Lyon. February 3.
New Zealand won by two goals, two tries and a penalty (23) to two tries (8).
Weather: Dry and cold. *Ground:* Firm. *Crowd:* 12,334.
Scorers: French Under-23: Philliponea and Bertranne tries. New Zealand: Batty (2), Stevens, and Wyllie tries. Karam two conversions and one penalty.
TEAMS:
FRENCH UNDER-23: H. Cabrol; S. Philliponea, R. Bertranne, J. Maso, A. Dubertrand; J. L. Berot (capt.) M. Pebeyre; J. L. Martin, R. Clerc, J. Ordioni, B. August, C. Spanghero, M. Yachvilli, V. Boffelli, R. Fite.
NEW ZEALAND: J. F. Karam; D. A. Hales, I. N. Hurst, B. J. Robertson, G. R. Batty; R. E. Burgess, I. N. Stevens; G. J. Whiting, R. W. Norton, K. K. Lambert, A. M. Haden, P. J. Whiting, K. W. Stewart, A. J. Wyllie, I. A. Kirkpatrick (capt.).
Referee: A. M. Hosie (Scotland).

From the city of Lyons to the Central Districts and the 'City of Tyres', Clermont Ferrand, the home of Michelin tyres, a commodity badly needed in New Zealand where motor car spares are invaluable. The tourists were getting a little tired now; the hospitality was starting to take its effect, and several of the test side were rested, although 11 members of the side had appeared in internationals. The injured Going returned to the scene of activity to try out his injured ankle which went 'crook' in the second half of the Barbarians match. As it turned out, he would have been far wiser, both from his own and his side's point of view, to have remained in the stand and allowed the younger men, Stevens and Colling to have played in the last two matches. Going was to prove a dismal failure in the French test, which could well have been his last.

Thirty-first Match
Versus French Regional XV at Clermont-Ferrand, February 7.
New Zealand won by a goal (6) to a dropped goal (3).
Weather: Sunny. *Ground:* Firm. *Crowd:* 10,000.
TEAMS:
FRENCH REGIONAL XV: M. Driotecourt; J. P. Pudiabois, G. Anastique, C. Dadin, J. P. Gourdon; J. C. Roques (capt.), R. Astre; M. Reppelin, G. Fleury, J. Constantino, J. C. Rossignol, M. Sappa, J. P. Rives, A. Faillon, A. Dusang.
NEW ZEALAND: T. J. Morris; G. R. Skudder, M. Sayers, R. M. Parkinson, B. G. Williams; I. N. Stevens, S. M. Going (capt.); L. Clark, R. A. Urlich, A. McNicol, A. M. Haden, H. H. Macdonald, A. I. Scown, B. E. Holmes, A. R. Sutherland.
Referee: R. F. Johnson (England).

In the end, the All Blacks won this match by a goal to a dropped goal but in many ways it would be justice to the Frenchmen to say the tourists 'escaped', and that a comparatively unknown XV from the region, were more successful than the two previous sides at Tarbes and Lyons, who were much stronger on paper. Only one of the side, full-back Droitecourt, eventually played in the test, but he came on as a replacement for Cantoni when he was injured.

Yet these young players revealed the strength in depth of French rugby, probably greater than that of any other rugby country, and the All Blacks were glad to get out of the match with a victory. It was only their brave cover defence that saved them and, in this, Bryan Williams was truly outstanding. During the match Parkinson and Sayers had to be replaced by Hurst and Batty, and Williams moved into the centre. Unfortunately, once again, with Going and Stevens bent on nine and ten man rugby, these three-quarters had few chances in attack. The match disturbed the All Blacks because they had to struggle, but it also concerned the French selectors present, because they pondered on how the national XV would score against such a cover defence.

The All Blacks scored their try in injury time during the first half. Williams cross-kicked and Droitecourt misfielded the ball. Holmes and Haden were up to feed the ball back to Hurst who crossed for a try which Williams converted. In the second half, the French attacked strongly and scrum half Astre dropped a superb goal from 40 yards. Five minutes from time, Droitecourt kicked wide with a penalty attempt from 28 yards when he could have drawn the match. He attempted his kick in silence but, as always in France, the visiting kicks were taken to the accompaniment of whistling! So it ended in a 6–3 victory and a large sigh of relief from the visitors, but the French selectors must have left Clermont-Ferrand wondering what would happen on the Saturday at the magnificent Parc des Princes in Paris!

Sid Going declared himself fit after the match; fit yes, but not really match fit in the sense of the requirements of a full eighty-minute international, against a fleet-footed side. The All Blacks arrived in Paris, saw the sights, visited the night clubs, and were given a big show in the city's leading papers. People were told about the All Blacks and the fifty thousand tickets for the match were sold.

While they were in Paris, the N.Z.R.U., back in Wellington, issued a statement that the Springboks tour would go on. Only one player, Bob Burgess, announced that he was not available to play against them. Brewery workers in Auckland decided that the Springboks would get no beer in New Zealand. How quickly all these people forget the amazing hospitality extended to the All Blacks in South Africa in 1970, and that the team was managed by a brewery official! Again, the rugby men of New Zealand wanted the tour to go on but, before the match in Paris, the N.Z. Press appeared to be divided. Some said it would not take place. The N.Z. public were divided but a plebiscite would have brought a majority 'yes' for the tour, for rugby football is the N.Z. national game, and the Springboks would no doubt be better behaved under pressure than the Seventh All Blacks. They would be disciplined and uncomplaining.

The week of the match did not go well for the French. Walter Spanghero, the captain, wanted a squad training session on the Wednesday, but the Selectors would not agree. However, the team assembled on Wednesday evening and had a session on Thursday which was almost a disaster. Full-back Aguirre tore a hamstring and Barrau injured a knee, while Campaes twisted an ankle. The selectors moved Cantoni to full-back and Trillo was replaced by Lux in the centre but, by Saturday morning, Barrau and Campaes reported fit.

It rained hard on Friday and when the teams fielded to a barrage of firework rockets, the surface was soft. Every seat in the spacious stands was taken, and the Referee was Paddy D'Arcy of Ireland, one of the best in the Five Nations. I was delighted to see him in harness, after watching some indifferent refereeing in some of the tourists' other matches. The All Blacks fielded as selected and, though a little tired, felt they could do it, by employing the same tactics as in the four previous internationals. They did not think they would lose their unbeaten test record.

Thirty-second Match
Versus France at Parc des Princes, Paris, on February 10.
France won by two goals and a penalty (13) to two penalties (6).
Weather: Showery. *Ground:* Soft. *Crowd:* 50,000.
TEAMS:
FRANCE: J. Cantoni (*Beziers*); R. Bertranne (*Toulon*), C. Dourthe (*Dax*), J. P. Lux (*Dax*), A. Campaes (*Lourdes*); J. P. Romeu (*Montferrand*), M. Barrau (*Toulousain*); J. L. Azarete (*St. Jean de Luz*), R. Benesis (*Agen*), J. Iracabal (*Bayonne*), E. Cester (*Valence*), A. Esteve (*Beziers*), P. Biermouret (*Agen*), W. Spanghero (*Narbonne*) (capt.), O. Saisset (*Beziers*).
NEW ZEALAND: J. F. Karam; B. G. Williams, B. J. Robertson, I. A. Hurst, G. R. Batty; R. E. Burgess, S. M. Going;

G. J. Whiting, R. W. Norton, K. K. Lambert, P. J. Whiting, H. H. Macdonald, A. R. Sutherland, A. J. Wyllie, I. A. Kirkpatrick (capt.).
Referee: D. P. D'Arcy (Ireland).

Karam set the match in motion but his kick sailed dead. France should have scored after four minutes when Esteve was forced into the corner supporting a back movement which Lux and Campaes should have made into a try. Karam failed with two penalty attempts from 50 and 37 yards respectively and France should have got another try, only for Cantoni to hurt a leg dealing with an up-and-under. This was after 19 minutes and, if any one thought he was throwing a 'Hollywood' they were proved wrong ten minutes later, when he had to leave the field.

After 23 minutes, France deservedly took the lead. Spanghero gathered in the long line and dashed away before handing on to Barrau who made ground away from the defence to his right and sent Dourthe sailing through on a 25 yard run for the line and a fine try that Romeu could not convert. Two minutes later the four point lead was cut to a single point when Karam kicked an excellent 40 yard goal from the left amid intense whistling, after obstruction at the kick off during the restart of play following the French try.

Burgess then made a lovely break, taking the ball behind his back one handed and bringing it round to the front, à la Jeff Butterfield at Ellis Park in 1955. Bertranne saved bravely and then Cantoni left the field in agony, to be replaced by Droitecourt. Williams had difficulty in throwing in straight from touch and was eventually spoken to by Referee D'Arcy. Barrau was successfully harassing Going and eventually stole a heel from in front of the All Blacks' feet. Needless to say, this shook the tourists and delighted the crowd, who continued to whistle and shout and sing gustily, *Allez les bleus*. Who could blame them? The French were on top and looked like winning. Of this, there was no doubt, and the 'Big Three', Spanghero, Esteve and Cester, were in right royal form, charging through the line-out on to the All Blacks halves, while Saissett and Biermouret were everywhere. Barrau was impossible to suppress, while Romeau punted like Barry John.

The All Blacks were having trouble at the set scrums where

Whiting and Lambert as props were under pressure from hard rivals and, at the rucks, the tourists got little ball. Worse than that, their back row forwards were contained and Wyllie and Sutherland looked slower and more unhappy than ever before. It was a real day of reckoning for nine man rugby – when the All Blacks got the ball, not always going forward, it was kicked to touch by Going, Burgess or Hurst at second five eighth (inside centre). Williams and Batty were starved on the wings and, when they did get the ball, were not happy with its greasy nature.

In the third minute of injury time, France went further ahead when Spanghero slipped to Barrau at a set scrum and the scrum-half went to a rather wide blind side on the right. Spanghero went with Barrau and carried on the movement, before feeding Dourthe who was able to give Bertanne, on the right wing, the overlap and he went really hard for thirty yards and a try. The New Zealand cover wasn't going to stop him this time! A fine try and Barrau was in it again. Romeau kicked a good goal from the 25 line and it was 10–3 at the interval.

After eight minutes of the second half, Karam kicked his second penalty, a much easier one from the '25', when Biermouret fell offside at a scrum, to make it 10–6. There was just a chance that New Zealand would get right back into the game with another score but they did not have the pace or the energy to do so and Romeau, with his second attempt of the half (his first was from 58 yards), kicked a penalty 20 yards out when several All Blacks were inside the ten yard area at a mini line-out. This made it 13–6 with New Zealand needing to score twice to win, a task, obviously, beyond them, if the French did not concede any penalties. They did better; they penned the All Blacks in their own half, then ran at them and tested them with Romeau kicks, and the tourists grew leg weary. They just managed to cover but could not attack. France hammered away and the 'veteran' tourists began to look battle weary.

Going conceded another penalty and Romeau was just wide. Then it was all summed up when Sutherland just got back to gather and save, and get the ball gladly and desperately into touch. The final whistle went. The tour was over, and the All Blacks finished with a record below that of any of their predecessors. They had had their moments, but failed themselves and their country in many ways. It would not have been justice had they enjoyed a better record than Jack Manchester's men of 1935 or Bob Stuart's of 1953. They lacked the personality and strength of character of these previous teams.

I felt there would be much heart-searching when the tourists arrived home. The side lacked two things; dignity and discipline, invaluable aids to a successful tour. No one could tell them anything. They knew it all; at least they thought they did. Not all of them, but too many for the good of the side.

It could have been so different. The British wanted it to be a happy tour but the Seventh All Blacks were not prepared to meet anyone half way. I hope that New Zealand rugby will not suffer, as a whole, from the unhappy effects of this tour. They must persevere with the younger players and encourage them to run, and discipline those who believe they know it all. They must come again; in happier mood. We will be waiting with hands extended. Next time they must accept the hand of friendship and be diplomats on and off the field. The game is bigger than any player or any team!

APPENDIX 1: RESULTS AND DETAILS OF MATCHES

Note: First two matches of tour played prior to arrival in U.K.

					Points Scored									
No.	Date	Opponents	Venue	Result	G	T	P	DG	For	G	T	P	DG	Agt
3	Oct. 28	Western Counties	Gloucester	Won	4	3	1	-	39	1	—	2	-	12
4	31	Llanelli	Stradey Park	Lost	—	—	1	-	3	1	—	1	-	9
5	Nov. 4	Cardiff	Arms Park	Won	1	2	2	-	20	—	1	—	-	4
6	8	Cambridge University	Grange Road	Won	3	4	—	-	34	—	—	1	-	3
7	11	London Counties	Twickenham	Won	2	3	—	-	24	—	—	1	-	3
8	15	Leinster	Dublin	Won	1	2	1	-	17	1	—	1	-	9
9	18	Ulster	Belfast	Won	1	1	3	-	19	1	—	—	-	6
10	22	N.W. Counties	Workington	Lost	—	2	2	-	14	1	1	1	1	16
11	25	Rest of Scotland	Hawick	Won	2	2	2	-	26	—	—	2	-	6
12	28	Gwent	Ebbw Vale	Won	1	1	1	1	16	—	—	—	-	7
13	Dec. 2	WALES	Arms Park	Won	—	1	5	-	19	—	1	4	-	16
14	6	West Midlands	Moseley	Lost	—	2	—	-	8	1	1	1	1	16
15	9	N.E. Counties	Bradford	Won	1	—	—	1	9	—	—	1	-	3
16	12	Edinburgh and Glasgow	Glasgow	Won	1	1	2	-	16	—	1	2	-	10
17	16	SCOTLAND	Murrayfield	Won	1	2	—	-	14	—	—	2	1	9
18	20	Southern Counties	Oxford	Won	2	2	1	-	23	1	—	—	-	6
19	26	Combined Services	Twickenham	Won	2	1	4	1	31	—	1	2	-	10
20	30	East Glamorgan	Arms Park	Won	1	2	2	-	20	—	—	2	1	9
21	Jan. 2	S.W. Counties	Redruth	Won	1	6	—	-	30	—	1	1	-	7
22	6	ENGLAND	Twickenham	Won	1	—	—	1	9	—	—	—	-	0
23	10	Newport	Rodney Parade	Won	—	2	4	-	20	1	—	2	1	15
24	13	East Midlands	Leicester	Won	4	4	1	-	43	1	—	2	-	12
25	16	Munster	Cork	Drawn	—	—	1	-	3	—	—	1	-	3
26	20	IRELAND	Lansdowne Road	Drawn	1	1	—	-	10	—	1	2	-	10
27	24	Comb. Aberavon/Neath	Neath	Won	6	1	1	-	43	—	—	1	-	3
28	27	Barbarians	Arms Park	Lost	—	2	1	-	11	2	2	1	-	23
29	31	Selection A French XV	Tarbes	Won	1	—	2	-	12	—	—	1	-	3
30	Feb. 3	Selection Under 23	Lyons	Won	2	2	1	-	23	—	2	—	-	8
31	7	Selection Regional	Clermont Ferrand	Won	1	—	—	-	6	—	—	—	1	3
32	10	FRANCE	Paris	Lost	—	—	2	-	6	1	1	1	-	13
					40	49	40	4	568	25	16	37	5	254

Played 30 Won 23 Drawn 2 Lost 5

APPENDIX 2: APPEARANCES AND SCORERS IN GREAT BRITAIN AND FRANCE

								in France		*Totals*	
	Name	*Appearances*	*Tries*	*Cons*	*Pens*	*Dp Goals*	*Total*	*Appearances*	*Points*	*Appearances*	*Points*
1	T. J. Morris	8	0	5	11	2	49	2	1p	10	52
2	J. F. Karam	17	2	27	21	0	125	2	3p 2c	19	138
3	G. B. Batty	18	17	0	0	0	68	3	2t	21	76
4	G. R. Skudder	10	3	0	0	0	12	2	—	12	12
5	D. A. Hales	15	5	0	0	0	20	1	—	16	20
6	B. G. Williams	19	7	0	3	1	40	3	1p 2c	22	47
7	B. J. Robertson	11	2	0	0	0	8	3	1t	14	12
8	I. A. Hurst	12	6	0	0	0	24	3	1t	15	28
9	R. M. Parkinson	11	4	0	0	0	16	2	—	13	16
10	M. Sayers	13	4	0	0	0	16	1	—	14	16
11	I. M. Stevens	10	2	0	0	0	8	3	1t	13	12
12	R. E. Burgess	16	5	0	0	0	20	2	—	18	20
13	S. M. Going	16	3	3	0	1	21	2	—	18	21
14	G. L. Colling	12	2	0	0	0	8	1	—	13	8
15	B. Holmes	9	0	0	0	0	0	2	—	11	0
16	A. R. Sutherland	14	5	0	0	0	20	3	—	17	20
17	I. A. Kirkpatrick	20	5	0	0	0	20	3	—	23	20
18	A. L. Scown	12	1	0	0	0	4	1	—	13	4
19	A. J. Wyllie	16	4	0	0	0	16	2	1t	18	20
20	K. W. Stewart	10	1	0	0	0	4	1	—	11	4
21	A. M. Haden	14	2	0	0	0	8	2	—	16	8
22	P. J. Whiting	16	1	0	0	0	4	3	—	19	4
23	H. H. Macdonald	14	0	0	0	0	0	2	—	16	0
24	I. M. Eliason	9	0	0	0	0	0	1	—	10	0
25	K. A. Murdoch	8	1	0	0	0	4	-	—	8	4
26	G. J. Whiting	17	0	0	0	0	0	2	—	19	0
27	J. D. Matheson	9	0	0	0	0	0	-	—	9	0
28	K. K. Lambert	13	0	1	0	0	2	2	—	15	2
29	R. W. Norton	11	0	0	0	0	0	2	—	13	0
30	R. A. Urlich	15	1	0	0	0	4	2	—	17	4
31	L. Clark	5	0	0	0	0	0	2	—	7	0
32	S. McNichol	3	0	0	0	0	0	2	—	5	0